THE WINE AND CHOCOLATE EVACUATION PLAN

By Brenda Barnes

*Dear Marlene,
Get well so you can put this plan in action.
Love,
Brenda Barnes*

THE WINE AND CHOCOLATE EVACUATION PLAN
Copyright © 2009-2010 by Brenda Barnes. All Rights Reserved. Printed in the United States of America. No Part of this book may be used or reproduced in any manner whatsoever without written permission except in the case of brief quotations embodied in critical articles and reviews. For more information write Brenda Barnes, P.O. Box 382, Destin, FL 32540-0382 or visit www.wineandchocolateplan.com.

Shadow Press books may be purchased for educational, business, or sales promotional use. For information please write: Brenda Barnes, P.O. Box 382, Destin, FL 32540-0382 or visit www.shadowpresspublishing.com.

Cover and Book Design Copyright © 2009-2010 by Alison Rivas. For more information please write Alison Rivas, P.O. Box 11743, Burbank, CA 91510 or visit www.artintheweb.com.

Photography by Kimberly Barnes and Mike Coggins

*For my three L.A. friends: Cathy, Laurel and Ilene.
I promised I would write it down.*

Contents

Acknowledgements   7

Introduction   9

Part I: The Plan - *The most important thing to remember!*   17

   1. First Things First - *Where do I start?*   19

   2. Transportation - *Should we take one or two cars when we evacuate?*   25

   3. Baggage - *How should I choose what to take with me?*   29

   4. Documents - *What important papers should I take?*   33

   5. Relief vs. Regret - *Is it really worth all the effort to pack my things for an evacuation?*   39

   6. Measuring Your Transport Space - *My family always ends up in a big fight when everything we have packed doesn't fit in our car.*   47

   7. Evacuation Packing 101 - *I have been packing my entire life. Why should I learn your system?*   53

   8. Clothing - *I think you are crazy to tell people to pack a business suit when evacuating.*   63

   9. Packing Limits - *When have I packed enough?*   69

10. Securing Your Home and Valuables - *Is there anything I can do to help protect what I leave behind?*   73

11. Extra Credit Evacuation Preparations - *What are some fun wine and chocolate activities to prepare for evacuation?*   87

Part II: Special Considerations   **95**

12. Evacuating Children - *How can I keep my kids safe during an evacuation?*   97

13. Evacuating Pets - *What should I know about evacuating my pets?*   103

14. Evacuating the Elderly - *How do I care for elderly family members during an evacuation?*   107

15. Evacuating from Out of Town - *What do I do if I am not at home during an evacuation?*   111

Part III: The Party - *Why you should host a party!*   115

16. Timeline   117

17. Advance Party Preparations   119

18. Twenty-two Steps to a Perfect Party   123

19. Sample menu and Recipes   137

20. Decorations and Shopping List   145

Checklist for an Evacuation - *A step-by-step guide for an actual emergency.*   149

Postscript - *I have a great idea that you should put in your book.*   153

ACKNOWLEDGEMENTS

I would like to thank everyone who helped to make this book a reality. I'll start with the countless women who have been kind enough to share their evacuation stories with me during the years. I appreciate the honesty and courage it took for some of them to tell me of their more painful experiences. Thanks to Blandy and Pam who were the first to listen to my "wine and chocolate" angle at dinner one night. Alison Rivas, Doctor Roebuck, Elizabeth Roebuck, Cathy Cobin, Gini Coleman, Liz Empson, and Ellen Zamorano are all smart people who were generous enough to read my manuscript and offer valuable advice. Any mistakes contained therein are my fault and were made despite their best efforts. I also want to thank Robyn and Jon Fink for sharing both their wine and artistic vision. I am grateful to my family for their support, love, and encouragement during the writing experience: my husband, Frank; my daughter, Alison; and my mother, Marjorie. Thanks to Hillary, Briane, Sarah K, Terri, Erin, Margaret, Vickie, Rita, and Amy for agreeing to participate in the very first focus group. The original Destin Book Club Members, Mistei, Terri, Ellen, Patty, Jay Gee, Liz, Mandy, and Tracey for loving my ideas and doing everything possible in assisting me from the beginning of this process. These ladies are my heart sisters and I love them. As William Shakespeare said, "I am wealthy in my friends."

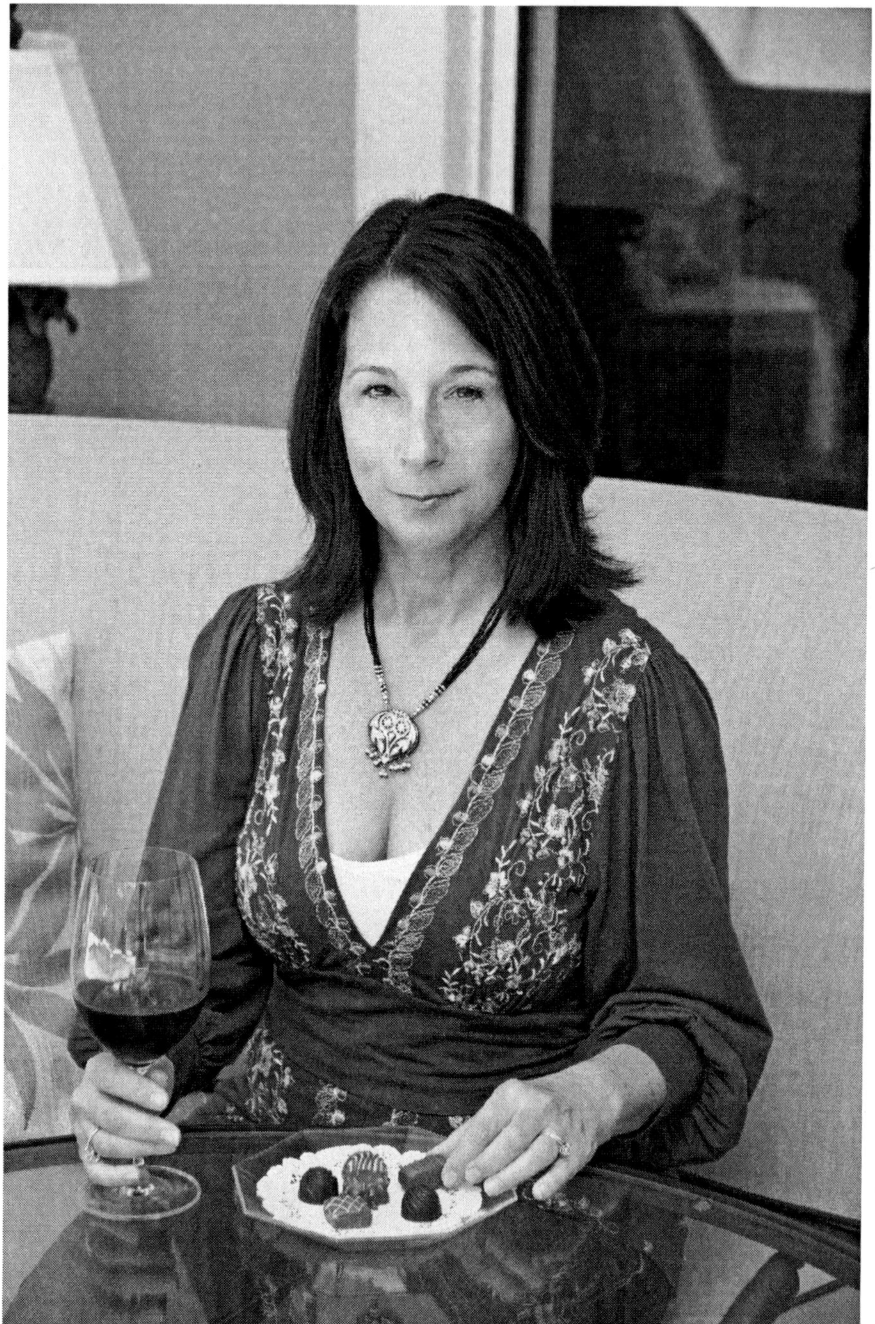

INTRODUCTION

*What made you want to write this book,
and why wine and chocolate?*

When the California fires hit in 2007, they were an emotional hit to my heart. My heart literally hurt. My daughter and three good friends lived in Los Angeles. What possible good was all the experience and practice I had in evacuation going to do them? I called and tried to give them advice over the phone, but this simply was not good enough. I knew I had to share my evacuation ideas and plans with, not only my friends and family, but everyone else. As more and more people are forced to flee in the face of escalating disasters, I want them first to evacuate (because it is stupid not to) and secondly, evacuate smarter.

I am certainly not a survival or disaster expert. In fact, I am the exact opposite of those wonderful, capable people. I have told my family for many years, "If I ever get lost in the woods do not call off the search at dark because I'm afraid I wouldn't make it till dawn!" The glaring omission of a survival gene in my DNA became particularly worrisome when my husband moved our family to the gulf coast of Florida in 1980. I realized I was now living in a stretch of Florida where hurricanes regularly come and make destructive visits. I had nightmares about my children being blown away by a fierce wind. So I decided to figure out

The Wine and Chocolate Evacuation Plan

a way to fight the hurricanes which kept hitting my area. First I evaluated myself. I did the exercise where you take a piece of paper, draw a line down the middle, and then list strengths on one side and weaknesses on the other. I was concerned when I finished my evaluation because the list under weaknesses was much longer than that for strengths. Next, I took out a piece of paper for my opponent—the hurricane. The strengths of a hurricane were overwhelming and went on forever, but I could not think of a single weakness. That is when I finally got it! There is no way to fight a hurricane! The only possible choice was to get out of its' way.

When you give this some thought this is true of all natural disasters. You cannot fight an earthquake, a tornado, a hurricane, or a flood. In fact, the only natural disaster which can be fought is a wildfire. Even with fire the vast majority of us still need to just get out of the way. We need to let the professionals do their jobs without having to worry about us. These professionals are called firefighters. There are no professional hurricane, earthquake, flood, or tornado fighters. The reason these words do not exist is because these actions cannot be done.

So what was I going to do? I faced an opponent who was guaranteed victory because I could in no way change the impact or course of the approaching force of nature. I realized that my only hope was in running away fast. Yes, I could prepare by putting up shutters or sandbagging but when the disaster approached my best odds were in running away.

This was the beginning of my journey to becoming a "personal evacuation expert." If anything makes me special it is my ability to pack up my cherished belongings and leave my house quickly. I shine in this category and can teach you how to do so.

There is a real chance you and your family will have to evacuate at some point in your life. I'm not trying to scare you but this is the reality of the times we now live in. It is a time of natural disasters which have increased in both intensity and scope and have resulted in mass evacuations. Some recent evacuations in the United States include: 2.4 million people evacuated from Houston, Texas in 2005 for Hurricane Rita; the 2007 Southern California wildfires forcing more than 800,000 people to evacuate; and at least 1.9 million people to evacuate from coastal Louisiana before Hurricane Gustav in August 2008. Category four and five hurricanes are becoming more commonplace. Fires are now becoming mega fires. More and more people have to evacuate and most are ill prepared in knowing how to do so.

My plan will prepare you and your family for any type of evacuation. I feel I am uniquely qualified to teach you how to do this quickly and efficiently based on my geographical location, education, and work experience. So please allow me to explain starting with my geographical location. Most of my adult life has been spent in the panhandle of Florida which is an active hurricane area. I have had to evacuate frequently, and have made a lot of mistakes in these evacuations which I have tried to learn from. Each time I evacuated, I would try to evacuate smarter. Over the years, I came up with a plan that has worked well for my family.

My educational background is in nursing. I went straight from high school to live in a hospital nursing dorm where I received my nursing diploma. I later went back to a university and received a Bachelor of Science degree in Nursing. Truthfully the diploma or the degree is not the thing which will make me valuable to you. What is important are my character traits and training which I developed during the process of becoming a nurse. I want you to think about this question. Have you ever known a nurse who was not just a little bit bossy? I am not being mean because after all I am talking about myself, and the nature of the worldwide nursing tribe to which I belong. Bossy is essential when you are trying to get people to do what they need to do quickly. It is especially good during stressful times when many people freeze up, or at least have much trouble focusing. This

The Wine and Chocolate Evacuation Plan

is why military, law enforcement, and medical personnel give firm blunt instructions. I will use my bossy nature to your full advantage when getting to the panic section of this book. Another helpful nursing trait is our profound pessimism. The nice nurse might be smiling and telling you everything will be just fine, but behind the smile is a sharp brain planning what should be done if the situation worsens.

Certainly nurse's sore feet can be a very beneficial thing for you to learn from. Why? Because a nurse learns early to keep the most essential supplies and information on her person so additional steps won't have to be taken to retrieve them when needed. A nurse knows how to plan, gather, and transport the necessary supplies to the necessary place in one trip. A nurse has been trained in organizational and execution skills. These traits are invaluable in an evacuation. So I prefer to think of myself as an assertive, forward thinking, and well prepared individual rather than the bossy, pessimistic, and sore footed old nurse, as some unkind people might choose to describe me. Whichever description you should choose to believe, people like me are just what you need in emergencies.

As to my work experience, I am a retired nurse whose career covers a period of 20 years. The last six of these twenty years I worked as a community health nurse in Florida. Part of the community health nurse's job description is to work in emergency shelters opened during disasters. I learned a lot from medical personnel and evacuees I met in these shelters. I learned that possessions with an emotional attachment were what most people grieved about leaving behind. I thought deeply about this and revised my evacuation plan to include emotional elements. When hurricane Andrew hit Miami, I volunteered to go there and work. I saw a lot of misery and great destruction while there. In the aftermath of this powerful storm, I kept seeing some familiar objects which had often made it through the disaster. Somehow I knew this was an important observation. When I returned home

Introduction

I kept seeing many of these surviving objects in my mind. Finally, I understood how I was meant to use this information, and once again I revised my evacuation plan. The plan is now ready to be shared with women everywhere. My mission is to teach you how to evacuate quickly with the things you love best.

Of course, you might only want to listen to me because I am going to encourage you to eat chocolate and drink wine. Yes you read this correctly. After completing certain of my recommendations you are encouraged to get a piece of chocolate, and pour yourself a glass of wine. (I challenge you to find another book that makes this recommendation in a bookstore. All you will find are those how to be skinny books.) I will make you work for your wine and chocolate but will support your right to savor the experience.

I first got women to listen to my evacuation plan by using wine and chocolate as enticements. For a long time I had tried talking to them about how to become better prepared for evacuating themselves and their families. Truthfully most women did not want to hear about it. The thought of having to flee from a natural disaster and possibly lose their home and possessions was too upsetting to consider. Evacuation was not something they wanted to think about much less plan for. I was frustrated because I had valuable information to share, but I struggled with how to inspire a genuine interest in the subject. How was I ever going to help anyone if they refused to listen?

A solution to my dilemma was unexpectedly found one night while having dinner with a couple of friends. After the meal we were sipping our wine and awaiting the arrival of a chocolate dessert when the conversation turned to a recent disaster which had been on the news that day. I took this as an opportunity to discuss my experiences and ideas related to evacuations. In the past I had observed that everyone seems comfortable expressing sympathy for those distant people impacted by disasters and evacuations. However, when you narrow the conversation down

The Wine and Chocolate Evacuation Plan

to what we each need to do in case one day we are in the same situation as "those poor people" most everyone becomes uncomfortable. Usually people begin to look worried or guilty and the subject is quickly changed to a lighter topic. This time was different. I did not know what made that moment so different. Could the women have been mellow from the wine they were sipping? Perhaps they were not going to leave before they had a little chocolate? Whatever their reasons I saw an opportunity and started talking. I began by telling them some of the mistakes I had made during evacuations which made them laugh. I kept the conversation light and engaged them by going around the table and asking what would you grab while running out of your home. Somehow we ended up having a great discussion while drinking the wine and sharing the chocolate dessert.

Later I realized what made this encounter meaningful was having fun. My friends had a lot of fun and, without realizing it, learned some important evacuation skills. I thought back to how earnest and serious I had always been about this subject. It was no wonder women did not wish to talk about the subject. I am sure I had scared them to "death." (If you are one of those persons I tried to talk to about evacuations in the early days, I'm sorry.) Now I knew what I needed to do. I had to make evacuation planning a pleasant event. The wine and chocolate definitely had worked the first time. It is hard to have a bad time while you are drinking wine and eating chocolate, and so I used this tactic to convince women to come to my house and listen to what I had to say. The title of my book changed from, The Women's Evacuation Plan to The Wine and Chocolate Evacuation Plan.

Wine and chocolate does not suit every female group situation. Please feel free to substitute any other theme in place of the wine and chocolate. If your friends do not drink you should change to another appealing theme. Some alternatives to consider are tea and biscuits, coffee and sandwiches, popcorn and

Introduction

sodas, or smoothies and salads. The only factor which cannot be substituted is the fun factor. If you decide to host an evacuation party, make sure your guests look forward to it and have a good time. The important information and needed skills are incorporated into the party activities outlined on the website. All you have to do is log onto www.wineandchocolateplan.com and the party plan is available for free! So relax and have a great time whether you are attending or hosting an evacuation party.

Finally, I would like to say, "Thank you," to everyone who is learning and sharing the skills in my book. Hidden in the fun is critically important information that has now found a way out to help people.

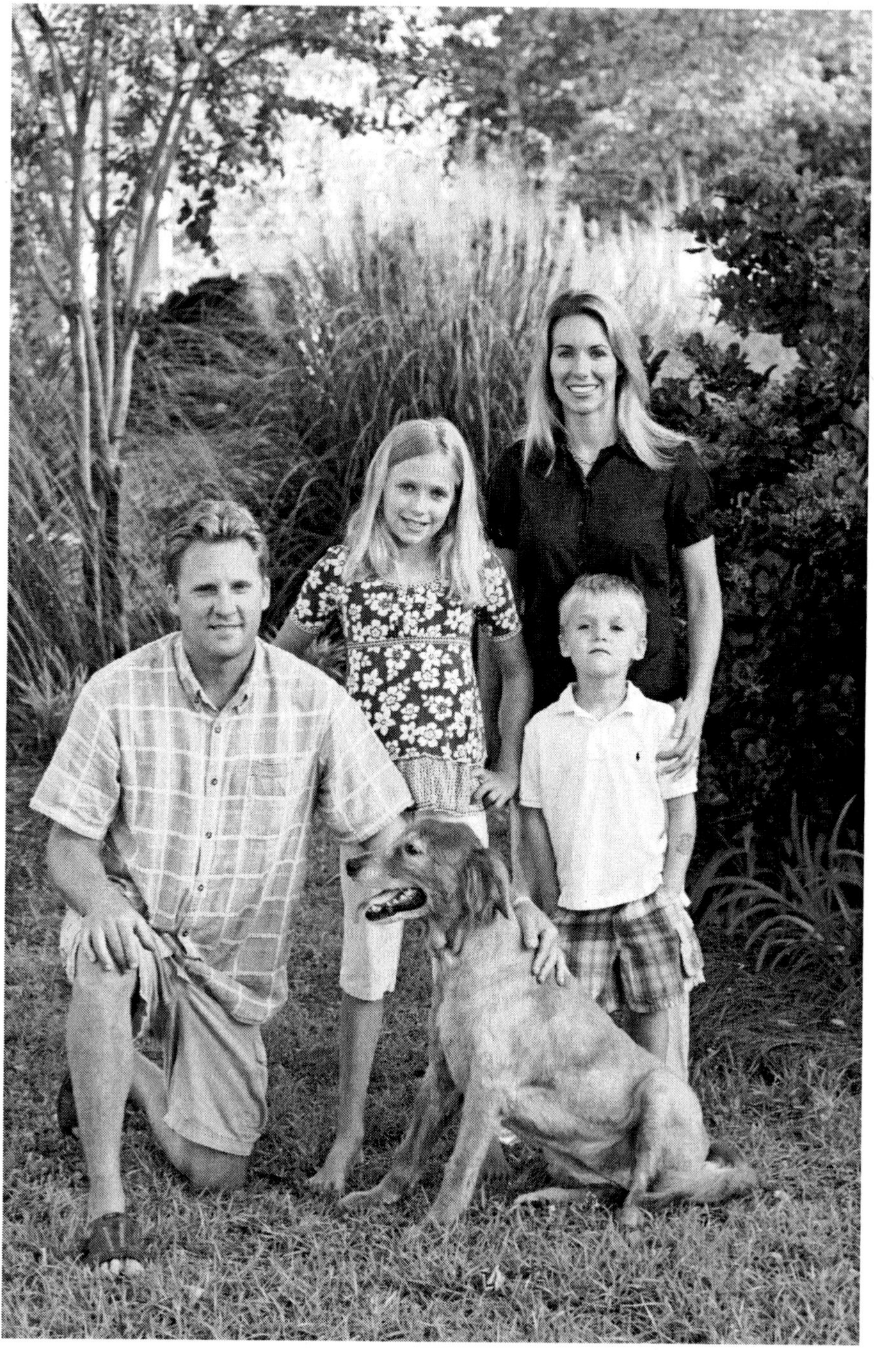

PART I

THE PLAN

What is the most important thing to remember in an evacuation?

The most important thing to know about an evacuation is that all living things in your household are the most precious items to be evacuated. Never stay or go back into a dangerous area for anything which does not breathe. If you lose everything you possess, but are able to save yourself, your family, and your pets, you have been successful.

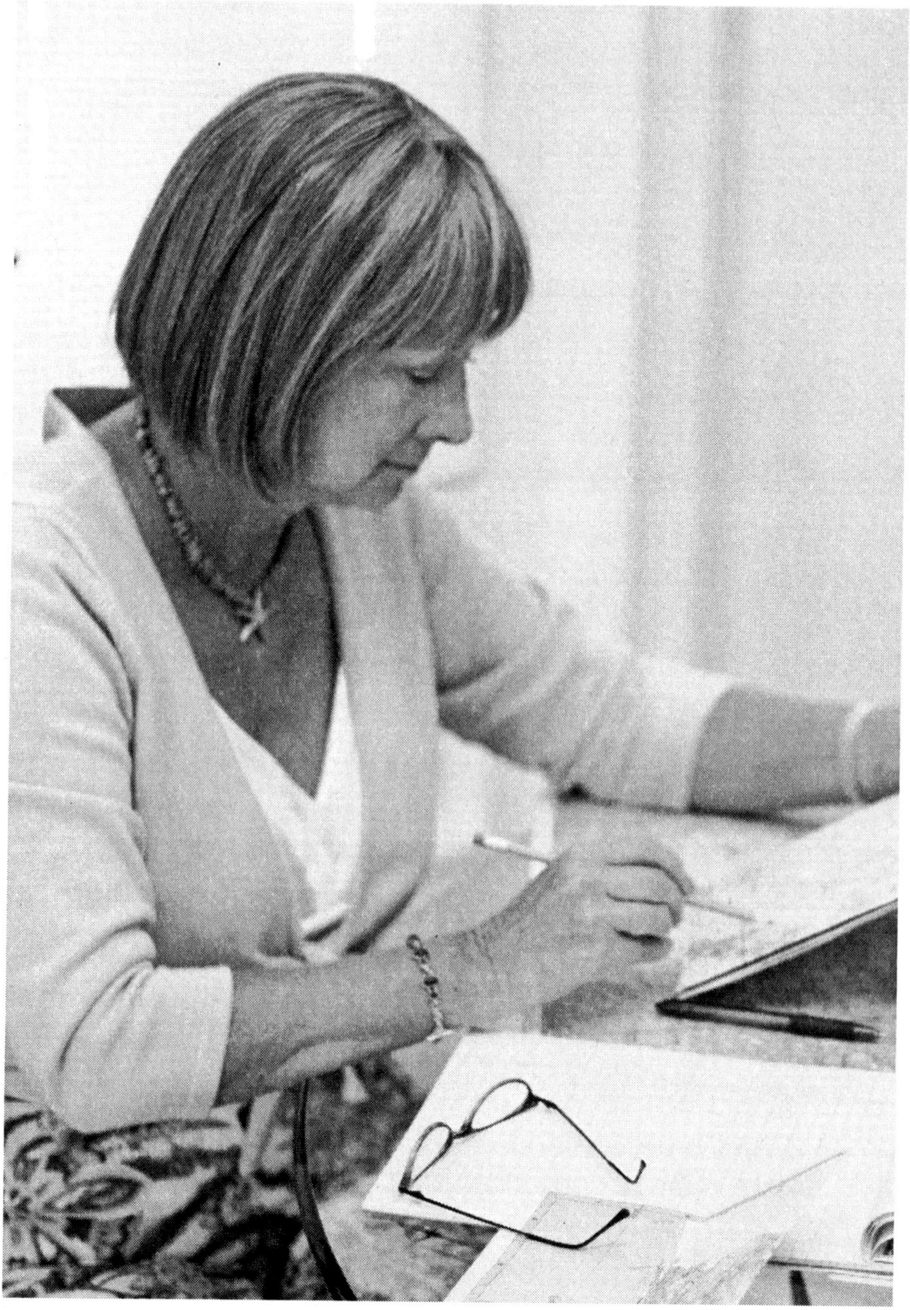

CHAPTER 1
FIRST THINGS FIRST

Where do I start?

Here is your first opportunity to earn some chocolate. After you have read and completed this section I want you to reward yourself with a nice chocolate bar of your choice. I bet it has been a long time since most of you have had a guilt free chocolate bar so let's get to work.

In order for you to get started in your evacuation preparations you must first decide where you want to end up. The choice of an evacuation location should be based on what disaster is coming and from which direction. You will want to travel away from the coming danger. It is also important to choose a place safe from the secondary damage which often follows a big disaster. For example, if your home is being flooded do not evacuate to a place situated down river. There is a good chance this spot will soon face a similar emergency and you will have you evacuate a second time. If at all possible try to pick a location where you will have some resources (family, friends, or work colleagues) to call upon if needed. It is wisest to pick out and plan for a trip of two possible locations. If you have prepared to use two different escape routes, you should choose the safest path, not just the one you are most comfortable with.

The Wine and Chocolate Evacuation Plan

If you will be staying in a hotel, I recommend securing a room in the selected evacuation locations as soon as a storm becomes imminent. When a hurricane is headed for the gulf coast of Florida, but landfall has not yet been determined, people should make reservations at two hotels in different directions. As soon as it becomes apparent where the hurricane will strike they should cancel the unneeded hotel reservation. It is important to ask each hotel the specifics of their cancellation policy to avoid any unnecessary charges. Of course it is nice if you have some family or friends you can stay with rather than in a hotel. If this is a possibility call them to confirm your stay as soon as possible.

I once had a young woman tell me that her family always went to an elderly aunt's house whenever they needed to evacuate. The woman said she just assumed that this is where they would always go. Then a big hurricane bore down on her home and she was unable to reach the aunt. Her family decided to go ahead and drive to the aunt's home anyway because they could not imagine her being anywhere else. However, when they arrived, the house was locked up tight and the aunt was definitely not home. The woman's family ended up having to drive a very long distance in very bad weather to find lodging. By the way, the elderly aunt who was never away from home turned out to be on a trip with her red hat club. While her niece was getting soaked on the road the elderly aunt was enjoying frozen umbrella drinks beside a pool. The moral to this story is you just cannot assume you have a space at a relative's home. You must call and confirm that there is indeed space available.

After you have selected the possible destinations you should plot two different routes to these locations. There are very often road closures during disasters due to wrecks, flooding, fires, smoke, bridge collapses, road washouts, high winds and a variety of other factors. If the primary route to your journey's end becomes blocked, you will need to be prepared for an alternative way. Do not allow any man you are traveling with make the navigational decisions. Most men refuse to admit they are lost and would certainly never demean themselves by asking for directions. Men want women to believe that they are the ultimate trackers and able to find anything. (This just cracks me up! Have you ever known a man able to find the mayonnaise in his own refrigerator?) Store completed road maps in the glove box of all family cars.

Now that you have two probable locations identified you must calculate the normal travel time for each. It is important to realize that you are definitely not operating in "normal times." The travel time will need to be doubled or even tripled to allow for the inevitable traffic jam which is sure to occur in these circumstances. This adjusted time is more realistic, and is what you should use as your latest possible departure time. This time will also need to be coordinated with the immediacy of the approaching danger. Mother Nature can change your best laid plans in a moment. If she should increase the winds fanning a wildfire, shift a hurricane's track, or cause the rain waters to overflow a levee your time of departure might be dramatically altered. You should always make safety the top priority when deciding what time to leave. Even with all the variables which might impact a departure, it is vital to have an estimated time of leaving in mind. The departure time is important because it will serve as a guideline for how much time you have to prioritize, pack your belongings, and secure your home.

Before you start to eat the promised chocolate bar please fill in the following blanks to prove you have really earned it.

The Wine and Chocolate Evacuation Plan

Evacuation Location #1_____
    Phone Number for Hotel or Family in area_____
    Hotel's Pet & Cancellation Policy _____

    Two Routes to #1 Location Printed and in the car (Just say, "I promise I did it" out loud.)
    Calculated Travel Time to #1_____

Evacuation Location #2_____
    Phone Number for Hotel or Family in area_____
    Hotel's Pet & Cancellation Policy _____

    Two Routes to #2 Location Printed and in the car (Once again say, "I promise I did it" out loud.)
    Calculated Travel Time to #2_____

When you have finished everything go and enjoy that lovely chocolate bar. You deserve it! The decisions you have made will save you precious time when you are faced with a real emergency. Congratulations! You have made a great start!

    (If you didn't finish and are thinking you can still have the chocolate bar, I'm sorry but no. I must warn you that should you eat it anyway you will develop two new cellulite bumps on your butt which will never ever go away.) After you have finished the chocolate bar, or finished pouting about not getting the chocolate bar, it will be time to address the next question.

Chapter 1: First Things First 23

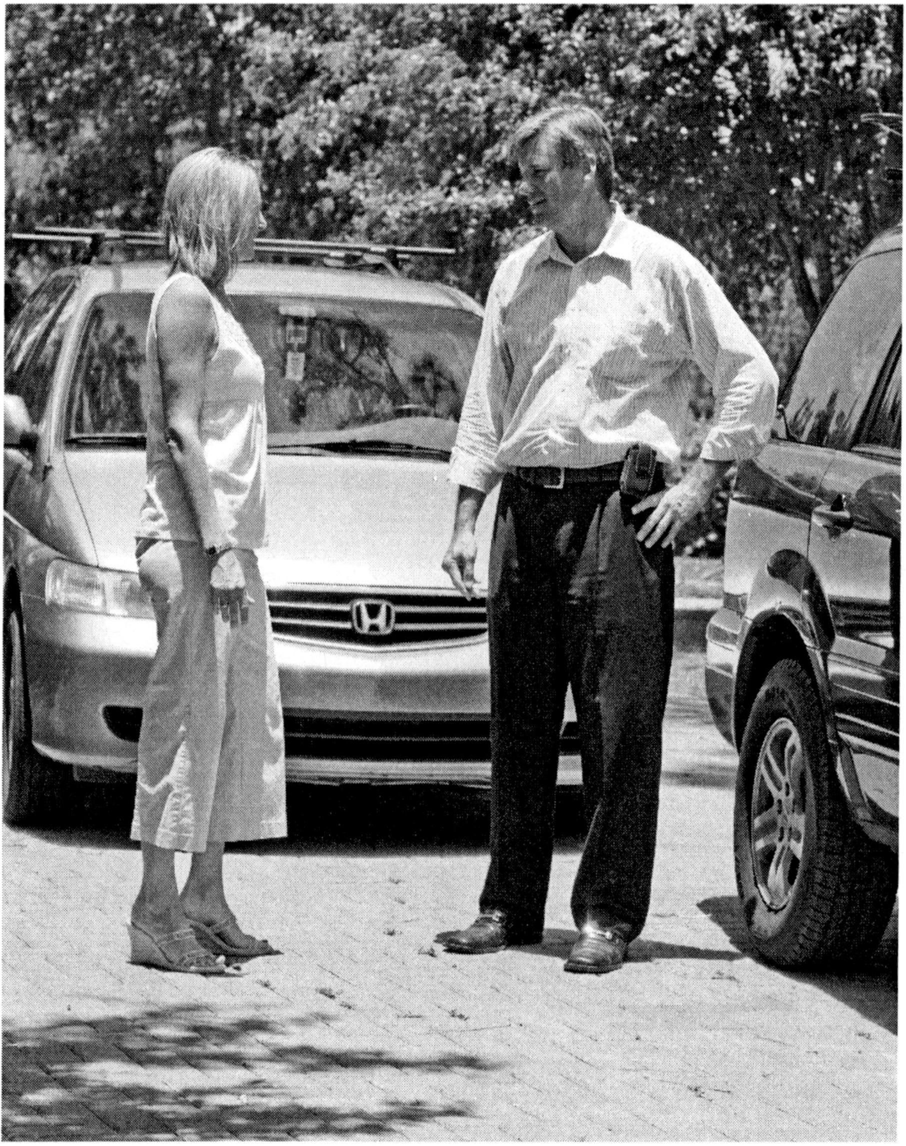

CHAPTER 2
TRANSPORTATION

Is it better to take one or two cars when we evacuate?

I realize that there are other modes of transportation which can be used to evacuate but the most widely used mode of evacuation is by car. The big question two car families always wrestle with is whether or not to take both. I'm not able to give you a final answer on this question. What I can do is give you the pros and cons of using multiple cars versus one car, and let you make an informed decision based on your personal circumstances.

I believe that for most people the single biggest advantage in taking one car is emotional security. During emergency situations it is human nature to want to keep your loved ones near. Personally I have found that this instinctive need for closeness diminishes with every mile I am forced to travel in a packed car with my family. I want you to be honest. Do all your family members get along, or do some of them immediately get into a fight? I am not naming any names but the policy in my family is to divide and conquer. The cost of an evacuation is also another huge consideration. It cost less immediate out of pocket expense to take one car compared with two. The cost of gas required for the evacuation trip will be half as much with one. This is not an insignificant factor when most families are trying

The Wine and Chocolate Evacuation Plan

to survive in these tough economic times. A lot of people worry that they increase the odds of being in a wreck or breaking down by taking two cars. What should be the most important factor is that you might have only one car which is suitable to carry you and your family to safety. The weather conditions and the sturdiness of the vehicle should be the most important reasons for taking one car.

If possible, I take two cars. (I know I said I wasn't going to give you a final answer but I did not say I wouldn't give you my opinion.) One of the most important reasons to take both cars is to keep them safe from the storm, flood, fire, etc. I want you to consider how much a car costs. A car is a big investment with wheels that can be moved to a safer location. Another advantage is that you are able to double your available transport space. This is a huge plus if you are faced with a serious threat to your home.

The magnitude of the danger you are facing must be carefully evaluated. If the situation looks bad, and you are able to take the second car, give it some serious thought. Following Hurricane Katrina many people from southern Mississippi and New Orleans came to the area I live in with only one of their cars. Following that horrible disaster the families had to make repeated trips back to the disaster area as well as try and establish a new existence in this new place. If either spouse was lucky enough to still have employment they had to go to work. My experience was seeing many of these displaced women struggling to rebuild a life for their families without any transportation.

You will save yourself a lot of grief if you will do the following exercise. If there is a significant other in your life, he or she should participate. I'm authorizing a glass of wine for all the adults involved. Now sip your wine and start to think of all of your daily activities which require the use of a car. You should quickly jot down the activities you think of on a piece of paper. The next step is to try and figure out how you could still do these tasks without a car. Is public transportation readily available in your area or in the area you are evacuating to? You must consider how a disaster would disrupt this service. Perhaps you have a friend or a family member who would lend you a car. How long do you realistically think you could keep the borrowed car? I have found when both spouses do this exercise they will usually decide in favor of bringing a second car. The husband only needs to hear that, if the worst should happen, his presence will now be required at every trip to the grocery store, every doctor's visit for the kids, every school activity, etc. and suddenly he understands the merits of taking a second car.

Discuss the decision you make and the reasons for it with the rest of your family well before the threat of any disaster. If the adults have already decided on this issue it will save everyone from an emotionally charged discussion during an already emotionally charged time. You have now figured out where you are going and how you will get there. I want you to pour yourself another glass of wine because we have now come to the agonizing decision of....

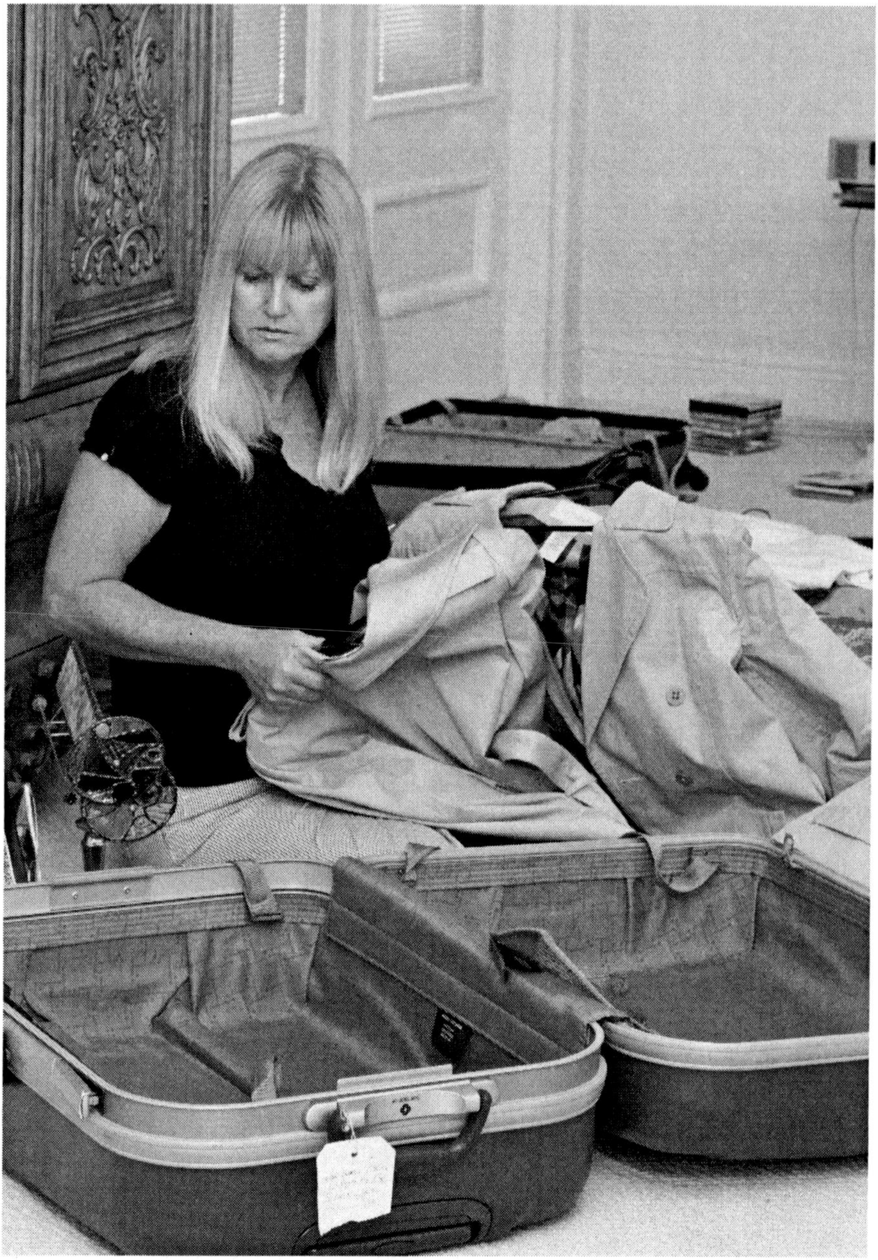

CHAPTER 3
THE BAGGAGE

How should I choose what to take with me?

I have given this question a great deal of thought through the years. Every person I have ever talked to after an evacuation for any length of time has eventually spoken of what they chose to bring, and what they regret leaving behind. It is amazing how many times I have been told, "I can't believe I forgot the thing which really means the very most to me." Well we all should believe that in the middle of a tense and hectic evacuation it is extremely easy to forget the things which are most important to us. It is essential to plan what items you would want to try and evacuate with you.

There are three important factors to take into consideration when you are deciding what to evacuate.

1. What is absolutely essential for me to have following a disaster should I lose everything?

2. What items are emotionally irreplaceable to me?

3. In the time I have, what do I have the capacity to carry out with me?

The Wine and Chocolate Evacuation Plan

We need to go over each of these three questions separately starting with the first question. What is absolutely essential to have following a disaster should I lose everything? I like to call this the brain-driven question because it has to do with important papers and numbers. In the aftermath of a disaster it is critical to have the correct documentation proving who you are and what you own. You then must be able to show additional documentation proving how you have insured yourself and your possessions. It is difficult to gather all of these important papers when you are trying to flee from danger. In fact, it is almost impossible to collect everything you should when you are under such extreme pressure.

I will illustrate how badly this last minute gathering of important papers can go by telling you about my personal experience. I was a young wife and mom in the middle of trying to pack my family up and leave before a hurricane hit. In the midst of my frantic activity a calm TV person informed me to, "Gather your important papers and evacuate the area immediately." What?! When this happened I was already in a state of panic, and my brain could not process what constituted "important papers". I did try to locate the "important papers" in between going out in the rain to help my husband move and secure something, and trying to calm down my kids who were running around screaming in nervous excitement. Once I returned from the hurricane evacuation and unpacked, I was very upset to see what I had considered vital documents. In my zip lock baggie of important papers I had my children's immunization records, their school's handbook, my telephone-tree list for their classes, a library card, my unpaid bills (which had been lying on a counter as I ran through the house), and a stamp card just two short of a free smoothie.

What I learned from this experience is that one, even me a personal evacuation expert, cannot be trusted to gather important papers during a crisis. I do not want you to make the same mistake I did. It is much better to think about it in advance and make up a check list. Since I know you are never going to do this I have taken the liberty of doing most of your homework for you. The following is a check list with fill in the answer blanks. Fill this out and you will already be better prepared for whatever disaster comes your way. You will receive extra credit in the real life evacuation test if you can identify and add other important items, names, and phone numbers. Once the list has been filled in be sure to keep this book in a very visible location in your closet, and take it with you when you evacuate. Of course I recommend you have the original papers collected and stored for the evacuation but the recorded information in the book will be a back up.

I add a special note about the first item on the list. It is the most basic first step in most proceedings but so elemental that we often forget about it. You have to prove who you are and how other people in your family group relate to you. It is not good enough to just say your name or even have another person vouch for your identity. All agencies will want some concrete verification to establish your identity before allowing you to access your bank funds, file an insurance claim, travel back into a disaster area to inspect your property, get on an airplane, rent a car, cash a check, and on and on. We usually rely on our driver's license as a quick form of identification. While the driver's license is a good place to start I can remember many evacuees whose wallets were forgotten, misplaced, or stolen during the confusion of an emergency situation. If your wallet is lost during normal times you can return to your home and dig up additional verification, but what would you do if there was no longer a home to return to? It is also possible that you will have to prove that you have custody over the children in your care or guardianship over the elderly people traveling with you.

The following list of documents is a long one and I recommend you allow yourself a week to gather, copy, and safely store these important papers. I don't want to hear any grumbling because there is a lovely surprise for those of you who are able to finish the task. No I can't tell you now because it is a surprise. You should just work your way to the bottom and I'll meet you there.

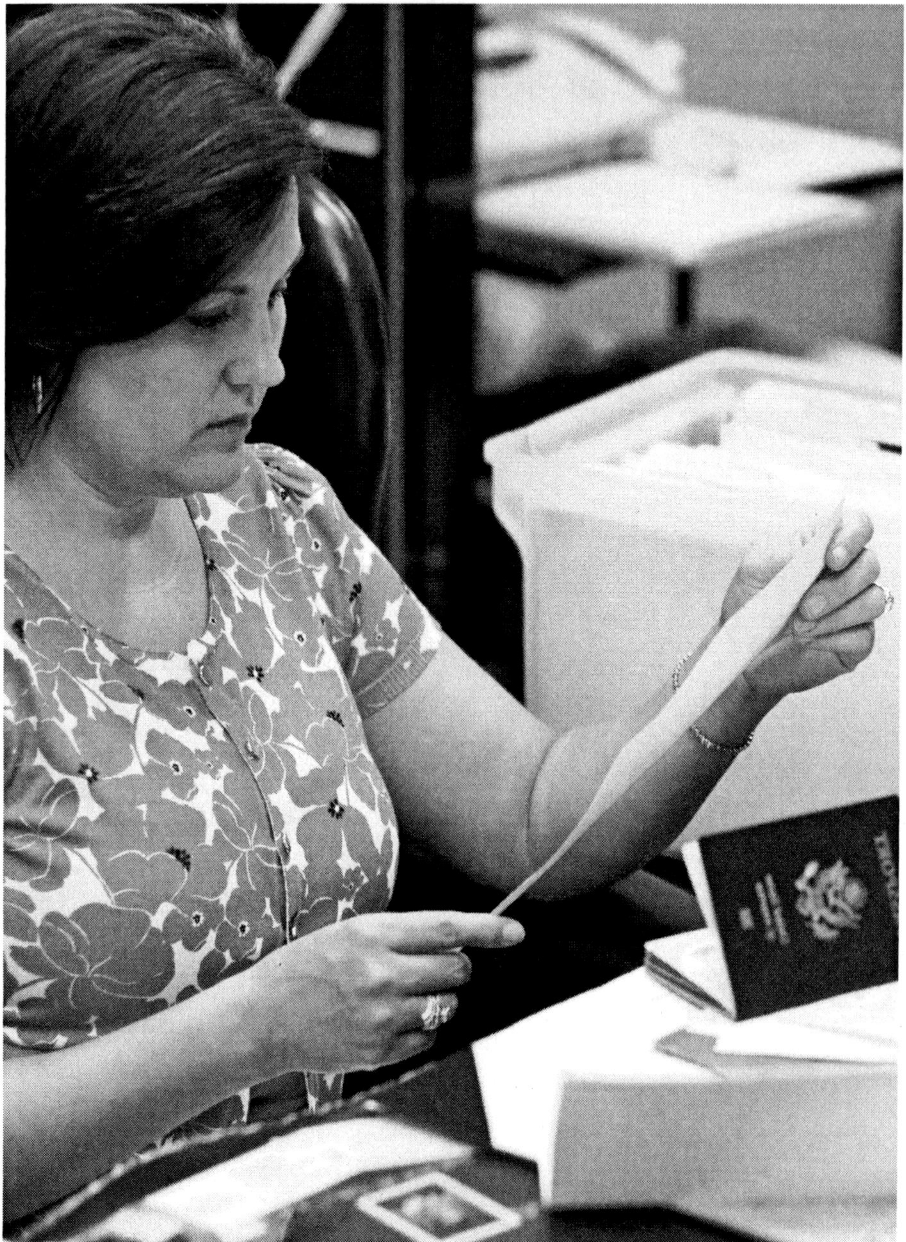

CHAPTER 4
DOCUMENTS

What important papers should I take with me?

If any account numbers require pin numbers or passwords please record them in a separate secure location.

A. Identity Papers
   Passport and Passport Number _____
   Birth Certificates_____
   Marriage Licenses_____
   Divorce Decrees_____
   Child Custody Decrees_____
   Guardianship Papers for Elderly Family Members_____
   Social Security Numbers_____
   _____

B. Homeowners Insurance Policy
   Policy Number _____
   Agent's Contact Number_____
   National Customer Information Number _____

C. Health Insurance Policy (or at least your I.D. Card)
   Insurance Number _____

The Wine and Chocolate Evacuation Plan

    National Customer Information Number_____

D. Auto Insurance Policy (or at least your I.D. Card)
    Policy Number _____
    National Customer Information Number_____

E. Any Other Insurance Policies_____

F. Bank Information
    Local Bank Telephone Number _____
    Checking Account Number _____
    Savings Account Number _____
    Safety Deposit Box Keys & Number_____

G. Credit Card Information
    Company Phone Number_____
    Account Number_____
    _____
    _____
    _____
    _____

H. Other Financial Information
    IRA Statement – Policy Number _____
    Stock or Bond Market Statement – Account # _____

I. Copy of Will & Medical Power of Attorney _____

J. Deed _____

K. Contracts_____

L. Professional or Business License_____

M. Medication – Rx's# _____

Chapter 4: Documents   35

N. Eyeglasses Rx#_____

O. Immunization Records_____

P. Pharmacy Phone #_____

Q. Doctor's telephone number _____

R. Dentist's telephone number_____

S. Veterinarian's telephone number _____

T. Photographs of family members_____

U. Photographs of pets_____

V. Phone Numbers of Family and Friends
_____
_____
_____
_____

W. Household Inventory List or Video _____
_____
_____

X. Cash_____

The last item is paper too many of us have forgotten to carry. It is CA$H. During disasters technology often goes down. Your credit or debit cards might not work. If this should happen you will need cash.

The Wine and Chocolate Evacuation Plan

The good news is that all of the preceding information can be gathered well in advance of any emergency. I realize not everything on the list can be taken care of by recording a number beside the listed item. When this is the case you should make a copy of the document and store it in a portable water safe container along with all the other similar documents from the list. I use the large sized zip lock baggies and it works just fine. Keep all of the collected items stored in a safe location where you can quickly retrieve them prior to leaving for an evacuation. Just like the storage of *The Wine and Chocolate Evacuation Plan* it is important to choose one place for this information to (always) be kept. If you move either the book or the document container from place to place you could waste valuable time trying to locate them.

Wow! You have really made it to the end. I bet you are feeling a great deal of peace of mind about how much better prepared for an evacuation you have become. Well you should feel proud. The effort you put into compiling and storing the above list will save you and your family a tremendous amount of effort and misery should a disaster strike. You should take the day off and go out for the luxurious lunch you have planned. Yes, I know you couldn't stand it and skipped ahead to read about the promised "surprise". How else would you already have reservations at the fancy restaurant? If you should want to pretend you did not cheat, or perhaps review the conditions of the surprise, go ahead and reread the next paragraph.

The promised surprise is ready to be claimed by the hard working woman who has completed the above list. A just reward must be given for the extensive and exhaustive work you have put into assembling all the vital paperwork. I think a leisurely lunch out with a girlfriend is exactly what is called for. I'm sure you will want a lovely glass of wine while you linger over the meal. When the waiter brings the dessert menu be sure to share a decadent chocolate creation with your friend. I want you to come home feeling rested and ready to tackle the next section of the plan. You will certainly need all your stamina because you must now decide on which of your possessions you will save and which must be left behind.

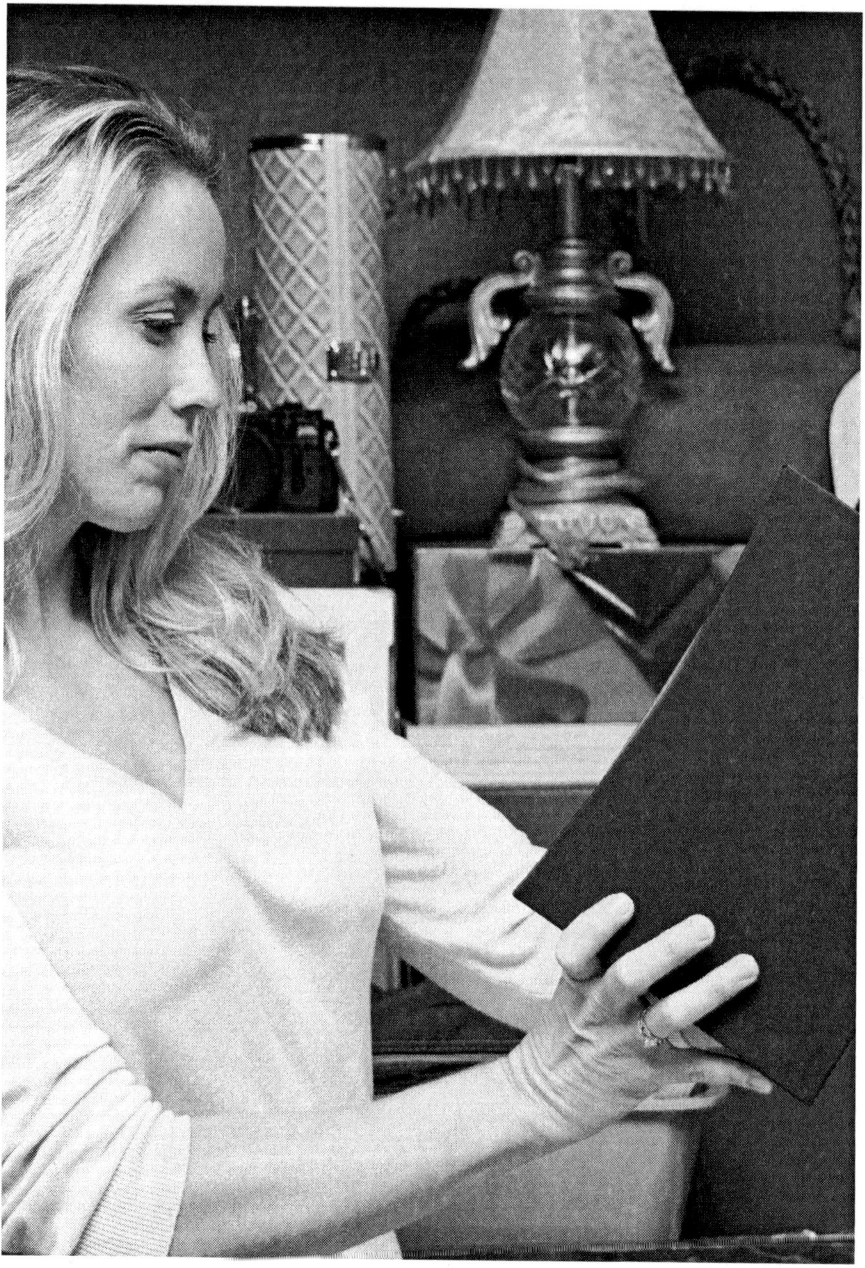

CHAPTER 5
RELIEF VS. REGRET

Is it really worth the effort to haul my things along during an evacuation?

I am asked this question a lot. I think it is because where I live we have to evacuate more than in most places. People can simply get tired of the work required in loading and then unloading their possessions. I certainly understand how they feel because I am often right there loading and unloading along with them. Everyone views having to quickly move their possessions during an evacuation as an unwelcomed chore. Still we must do so to safeguard the most precious of our possessions. I passionately believe everyone should try and take their ten most cherished possessions with them each and every time they leave in an evacuation. I believe this because too many times I have had to witness the grief people experience when they finally understand that it is all gone. Everything is gone. They are devastated because ever little piece of their life that held a special significance or memory has now been obliterated. I never want this to happen to you. I want you to be able to evacuate the material things that matter the most to you faster and easier. Since you must do it I am here to show you how to do so correctly.

The key factor in successful evacuation packing is your attitude which can make all the difference. I have met a significant number of women who have a very hard time considering what items they would try and save if faced with an evacuation. These women can often be heard saying things such as, "I just don't think it will ever happen to me," or "I can't bear to think about it. I'll just deal with it when I have to." Denial and procrastination seem to be their mottos. I have come to believe that many of these women feel that any acknowledgment of the possibility of a disaster somehow makes them vulnerable. (Rather like the people who refuse to make out a will because they think it is bad luck.)

If you are one of the above described women then the absolute most important thing for you to do is get a new attitude. You must face your insecurities, extract your head from the sand where you have it buried, and make some concrete preparations. I want you to pause and consider how terrible you would feel if you did nothing and ended up losing a treasured family heirloom. You would not only be letting down the family member who gave it to you but also future generations to whom the heirloom should be passed onto. That would be a terrible shame and all because you couldn't be bothered; were too scared; or maybe were just too lazy to make a few fundamental arrangements. Are you feeling terribly guilty? If you are now riddled with guilt I am so glad! I am happy because the guilt emotion has a good chance of overcoming the scared feeling and propelling you into productive action. (Stop before any of you write me angry letters concerning my use of guilt. I want you to remember that you are either a mother or had a mother so you are very familiar with the use of guilt as a motivational tool and have probably used it yourself). I promise you that every act of preparation you complete will make you less and less vulnerable. It is very helpful to think of evacuation packing as a drill each and every time you do it. Whether you are just practicing how you would wrap something for transport in a quiet moment, or whether the fires are raging in a nearby canyon while you pack during an actual evacuation, you should act as if it is a drill. This frame of mind will keep you focused, calm and enable you to accomplish the critical tasks facing you.

Now that we have assumed this wonderful "can do" attitude it is time to make our list of the top ten items to take during an evacuation. I want you to focus all that positive energy into identifying the ten items in your home which mean the most to you. If any of you are still feeling guilty I am authorizing an emergency glass of wine and a large chocolate chip cookie to consume as you create your top ten list. Okay maybe that is not being fair to the well adjusted members of my reading audience, so wine and chocolate chip cookies all around. If it is at all possible, you should try to find a stress free, quiet time when you are really able to think as you consider what should go on the list. The first list you come up with is rarely your final decision on what to take, but it does give you a starting place to work from. Remember that taking your family and pets is a given. You have also already collected all your important papers for transport. This list should consist of the ten most cherished material possessions which are in your home. It helps to ask, "What items are emotionally irreplaceable to me?" This list should be heart driven. Please, when you make it do not listen to your brain. Instead listen to your heart. Everyone's emotional landscape is personal and varied. There is a huge difference between financial value and emotional value. If you must leave something behind, and possibly lose it, which price will be easier for you to pay? Remember, there is no right or wrong answer, only your heartfelt choice.

I understand that for many women there are never any quiet or stressless moments in their lives. Even a chaotic life should not stop one from making a top ten list. You will just have to be more creative about finding time to compose it. Keep a piece of paper and a pen in your purse or pocket at all times until the list

The Wine and Chocolate Evacuation Plan

is completed. Whenever you feel that some item must be taken with you, jot it down immediately. Carry the pen and paper with you into the toilet. Many women have told me this is the only time they have a few minutes of privacy and peace.

I offer you my personal list of top ten evacuation items as a sample. I will discuss the emotional feelings I have associated with each of these items on my list, and hope that after reviewing my list, you will be reminded of cherished items of your own to evacuate. My list is intended to be only a starting place for you to begin thinking about your own cherished items. Once again, assume you have all breathing things ready to go. Also, you will have already collected the essential items identified in question number one above. Now list the material items you love. Once you have made your final choices list them in the empty charts I have provided. I give you three charts to fill out with not only your items, but other family member's lists as well. There are blank pages at the back of the book available for additional lists or notes. It is essential to write down all these objects because if you do not; you will probably forget some. I know because I have forgotten and then been sick with worry because of my oversight.

Brenda's Top Ten Evacuation List

Item	Location
1. Jewelry	Jewelry box
2. Daughter's smocked dresses	Suitcase under bed
3. Wedding painting	Bedroom wall
4. Sentimental ornaments	Under my bed (packed)
5. Tapestries	Bedroom wall
6. Great-Grandmother's quilts	Master bathroom linen closet
7. Family photo albums	Library - bottom shelf
8. Sterling flatware	Dining Room
9. Statues	Living Room
10. Crystal champagne cooler	Dining Room

The Top Ten Evacuation List #1

Item	Location
1.	
2.	
3.	
4.	
5.	
6.	
7.	
8.	
9.	
10.	

The Top Ten Evacuation List #2

Item	Location
1.	
2.	
3.	
4.	
5.	
6.	
7.	
8.	
9.	
10.	

The Wine and Chocolate Evacuation Plan

The Top Ten Evacuation List #3

Item	Location
1.	
2.	
3.	
4.	
5.	
6.	
7.	
8.	
9.	
10.	

The locations of all ten items have now been noted. When rushed and worried I often forget where I have stored something. Actually, I often forget where I have stored something even when I am not. When time is critical you cannot waste ten minutes looking through closets for grandma's quilts. I have grouped the items' locations together according to the room where I can find them. It is helpful to gather your objects in such a systematic way. You do not want to (as I once did) make three trips to an upstairs floor for things when time is short. As soon as there is a possibility that you might have to evacuate pack up your top ten items and place them near the door from which you will be exiting. Should you have to leave quickly everything will be conveniently positioned for transport to the car.

Chapter 5: Relief vs. Regret

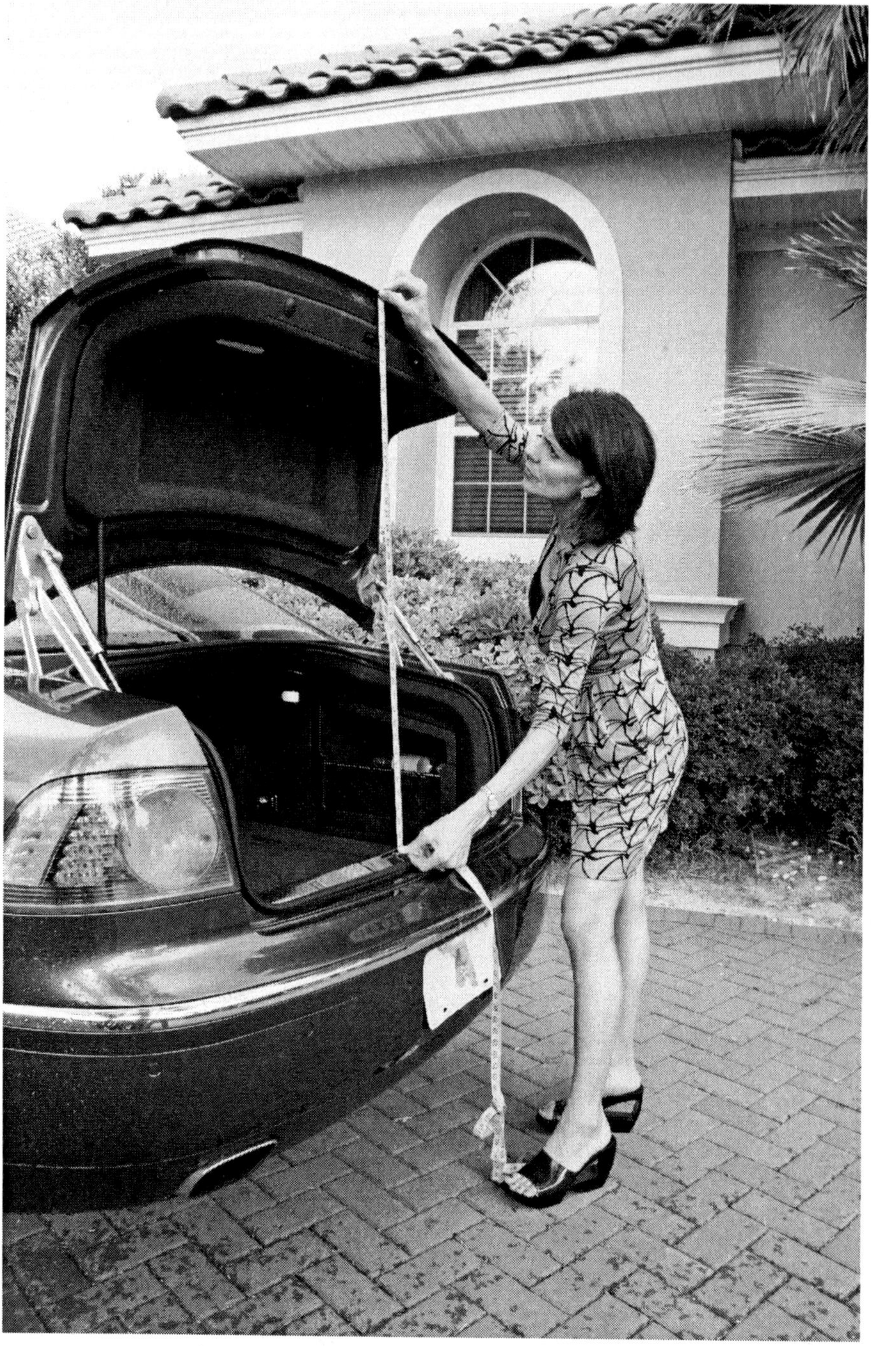

CHAPTER 6
MEASURING YOUR TRANSPORT SPACE

My family always ends up in a big fight when everything we have packed won't fit in our car.

I wish I could tell you that the above comment represents an isolated occurrence, but that would be lying. All too often when a family finally decides to evacuate each member will begin a frantic scramble for their valuable possessions. After locating their goods, each will rush their things to the car only to discover that the storage space is being filled up with everyone else's stuff! It quickly becomes apparent that the car will not hold everything. What usually happens at this point is that someone starts a heated discussion which always involves some other family member's valuables being "unnecessary junk." Of course this behavior leads to a loud rebuttal and a disrespectful description of the initial speaker's property. Soon you have a full scale family melt down. This is very dangerous because many times guns are part of the property being evacuated. Sometimes I cannot believe the things I have seen during evacuations. I once witnessed a couple screaming and throwing their possessions (some of which were breakable) at each other in the driveway while their child stood nearby crying. Another time an elderly woman at a shelter cried most of the night because her husband

The Wine and Chocolate Evacuation Plan

had angrily thrown a chain saw down on top of a cherished oil painting she had been trying to evacuate. The canvas was torn, and so was this poor old lady's heart. Stress can make people do terrible things. Stress can tear a family apart or can bring a family closer than they have ever been. Clearly understand that if all do not work together as a family during a disaster and evacuation, all are in very big trouble.

How can your family avoid such a dispute? This is just another way of addressing the third part of the overall question: "What should I bring with me?" "In the time I have, what do I have the capacity to carry out with me?" Believe it or not you have already dealt with a lot of the issues which could lead to the terrible scenes described above. You should have discussed with your family (and determined) which vehicle or vehicles you will be leaving in. By knowing which vehicle you will be leaving in, and the space you will have to share with others, you can determine how much transport space you will actually have. Measure your car's trunk space and any other space you will have for transportation with a tape measure. Write these dimensions down in this book because you might forget them before you get everything packed. If your family has decided to travel together it means you will not get 100% of the car's space for your things. Be prepared to sacrifice something to avoid a fight. I have a cradle my deceased grandfather made for me which I love because all of our family's babies have used it. It breaks my heart, but the reality is the cradle is simply too large to evacuate because it would take up every inch of space I would have in a large vehicle. Still it is good to identify such items so you can do your best to protect them before leaving.

Evaluate the section where you and your family (or traveling companions) have recorded the top ten items each of you would evacuate. If something must be left behind because of lack of transport space this should be discussed now before the pressure of an evacuation. Identify a problem in advance and discuss it. One lady I know on the gulf coast has some valuable antique furniture which she refuses to leave behind. This ingenious lady has the local U-Haul on her speed dial. At the first sign of a hurricane heading our way she has a truck reserved and family members signed up to assist her with the moving. This might sound a little extreme, but she has decided what she really wants to save, and has made a plan to accomplish her goal. She is my hero.

I leave some blank space here for you to record the storage dimensions of the cars or cars you will be traveling in. You must write all the pertinent measurements down. It helps me to sketch out the look of my trunk, and write myself little notes such as the indention where the spare tire is located. This drawing does not have to be completely accurate or pretty. It just has to help you remember clearly the space in which you will be loading your valuables.

CAR #1 STORAGE SPACE

The Wine and Chocolate Evacuation Plan

CAR #2 STORAGE SPACE

After each knows their space allotment, start packing. Close your eyes and mentally view the trunk's interior. Now visualize what you need to put in it. Evaluate which items should go on the bottom and which items should be placed on top. Perhaps you have a valuable painting with large dimensions you want to take. Before deciding to put it on the bottom consider how much weight will be placed on top of it. Also take into consideration how most trunks become narrower at the top. Now you have a mental sketch of how you will load your possessions.

Chapter 6: Measuring Your Transport Space

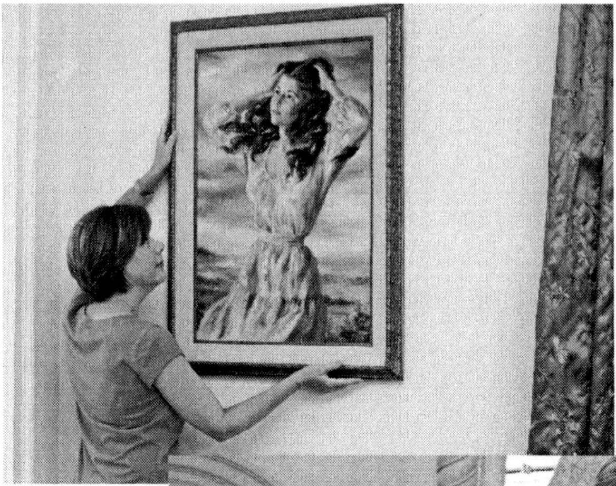

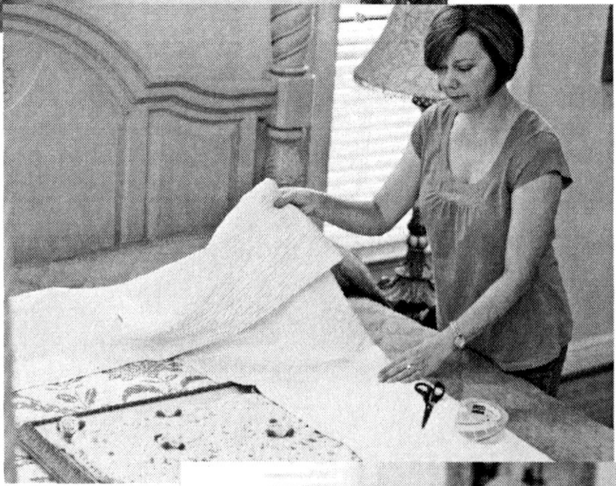

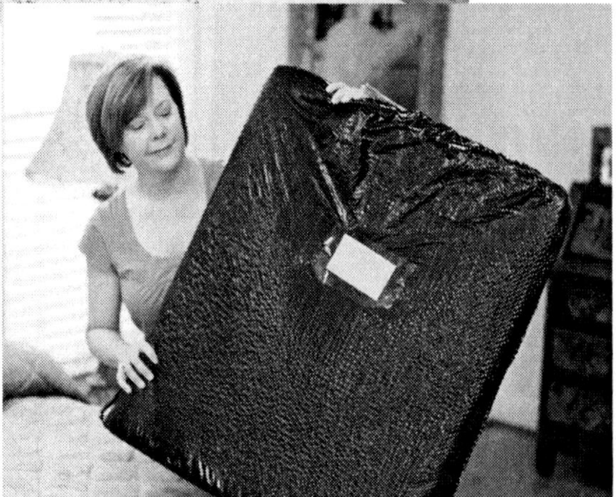

CHAPTER 7
EVACUATION PACKING 101

*I have been packing my entire life.
Why should I learn your system?*

You need to learn my system because evacuation packing is radically different from regular packing. The packing you do for an evacuation will probably be the most important packing you ever do. Every inch of transport space is valuable because the things you carry out with you might be the only things which survive the approaching disaster. Every minute you have to spend packing is critical because that is a minute's delay in your departure. My goal is to have you be able to pack your entire top-ten list, and have it in the car in less than one hour. This time frame might seem to be a bit daunting but with some thought, preparation, and practice you can accomplish it.

You have already done a great deal of preparation toward achieving a one hour packing time. The most important evacuation items have been identified. You have also already determined the space is available for transportation. This knowledge is a tremendous advantage in getting you and your things out of the house quickly. I have seen women spend thirty minutes walking around their house trying to decide what they should take. When leaving they have only managed to collect a few

The Wine and Chocolate Evacuation Plan

things because of their indecision. I understand why this happens. A lot of people just don't function well when life takes an unexpected turn and things become stressful. This is why you should make the big decisions in advance.

Buy a box of large sized garbage bags, a pair of inexpensive scissors, a pack of index cards, a roll of packing tape, and a marker. All of these items should be stored together in your home and only used during an evacuation. I recommend that these items be bought in secret, and then hidden somewhere far away from the greedy hands of other family members. After all how many times have you heard, "I meant to put it back" or "I was just borrowing it." You need to do the prudent thing and carry out the buying and storing of your supplies in secret. I keep my supplies bundled together and far enough under my bed so that no one is going to come across them by accident!

Before you pack one thing I want you to answer this question, "Do you really want to evacuate tissue paper, old newspapers and cheap boxes?" I certainly do not think you should include any of these items on your top-ten list. Why take materials which will just be thrown away after unpacking when you have so many useful items which will serve the same purpose? Instead of the standard packing items, go to your linen closet and take out your best sheets and pillowcases. Then go to your clothes closet and take out your favorite t-shirts, nightgowns, pants, and skirts. This will be your packing material. Should your home be destroyed you will need an extra set of sheets or a couple of extra outfits more than wadded up tissue paper. As you collect household items to use as packing material take the complete set--the complete set of nice towels, the complete set of sheets, the pants which go with the top, etc. If you are forced to start over it is much better to have a matching set of linens than to have odds and ends.

We will now do a mental packing with my top ten evacuation items. This exercise will help you to visualize evacuation packing in action. I hope by discussing my list you will begin to understand the emotional and financial components which factored into my selection of each item. You will see that safely packing some items proved a challenge, but was eventually solved. I have strived to consolidate my evacuation items during the packing process. By packing more than one evacuation item together I have been able to save time (by decreasing the number of trips required to load the car). Reducing the total number of packed bundles also aids me in keeping up with all my belongings during the confusion of an evacuation. After you have read through my process you will have a much better idea of how to pack your own list.

Ok, let's pretend the big fire, hurricane, or whatever is headed my way, and I must evacuate. So it is time to pack up the car. I take out my top-ten list. I have it written down because it is very hard to remember a list of ten things when anxious. I have also arranged these items in the order each will fit into my vehicle. Please notice that this order is slightly different from the original top-ten list. The first list was arranged according to the area of the house from which the items will be collected. The second list is arranged by the order in which the items will be packed and placed in the car.

1. Jewelry
2. Handmade baby dresses
3. Photo albums
4. Sterling flatware
5. Great Grandmother's quilts
6. Champagne cooler
7. Holiday ornaments
8. Statues
9. Tapestries
10. Wedding painting

The Wine and Chocolate Evacuation Plan

Item 1: Jewelry
I put on good jewelry that is not too fragile (no delicate chains or pearls). Even if it is a couple of necklaces, various bracelets and numerous rings that make me look tacky, I still put it on. My rational for doing this is that it's on my body so I should be able to keep up with it. Then I go to the closet and get a purse to hold the rest of the jewelry. As I put the jewelry boxes or cloth pouches inside the purse I count them. Then I write the number of jewelry containers inside the purse down on a neon index card and drop it inside. When I get around to unpacking this bag, I will usually have been through a great deal. The neon card will help me to remember how many items are inside the purse so none will be misplaced. If my purse is not full, I grab a pair of shoes that match the purse and stick them inside also. If I have one of those cloth bags that come with expensive purses I stick the purse inside. If I do not have a cloth bag, I will get a pillowcase, and drop the purse inside and tie it shut. Next I put the whole thing inside a small garbage bag, tape it shut, and label the whole bag with a neon card. I use the garbage bags to provide an inexpensive water proof outer wrap.

Item 2: Handmade Baby Dresses
Most I made for my daughter, but a few are my own baby dresses that my daughter also wore. These are emotional items for me. Every time I look at them I remember how much time, effort and love I put into learning how to do English smocking and French hand sewing. I think about the special occasions when she wore them and I almost tear up. I can't help myself, I am in my 50s and menopausal. I keep all of these dresses in a little suitcase under my bed. I thought, "I can just pull this out and put it in the car in a hurry." That was a pretty good plan. But then I came up with a better one.

One day while looking at my car trunk space I discovered the spare tire compartment. Yes, there is a spare tire there but also extra space around it, and more between the spokes. What a great place to transport something! I thought of the handmade baby dresses but I didn't want them messed up by the tire. So I put them in zip lock baggies and stuffed them around the edge of the tire and between the spokes. When I finished packing and replaced the spare tire cover, the trunk looked completely empty, even though, I had already stored something from my top-ten list. Many things could be stored in this manner. Any small fabric item like cloth napkins, handkerchiefs, t-shirts, etc. would work.

Item 3: Photo Albums
The third item on my list is photo albums which I store on the bottom of my bookshelf. So I only have to take them to the car, sealed in garbage bags and labeled.

Item 4: Sterling Flatware
My maternal grandmother took me to a jewelry store and had me pick out my sterling pattern on my tenth birthday. I am not making this up, she really did! From that time on I was always given a gift of sterling for Christmas, birthday, etc. When ten years old (or eleven, or twelve) this seems like a pretty lame gift. However as an adult I have come to cherish this sterling. I remember the trips where the two of us would go to purchase a piece with great fondness. I realize now that my grandmother always made these trips something of a special ceremony. She is gone but every time I use this sterling I remember her. I store the sterling in a silverware holder which has tarnish resistant cloth on the top, but no top to keep the flatware secure. When I am packing this item I put some pretty linen tablecloths on top of the drawer. I then take one of my great grandmother's quilts and wrap it around the entire drawer. Next, I place it all in a garbage bag, tape and label it and move on.

Item 5: Great Grandmother's Quilts
My number 5 item consists of my great grandmother's quilts. I just used one of these in wrapping up item number four. I will use the other quilts in wrapping up the last item.

Item 6: Champagne Cooler
My husband gave me a beautiful champagne cooler one year as an anniversary gift which I always take when evacuating. However, it is a large heavy crystal object that is difficult to pack. I have finally decided the safest transport for this object is in its original box which has foam cut-outs in the bottom that holds the cooler steady. What I do not like about using this container is the vacant space remaining around and inside the cooler after the box is packed. So I decided to place hand knitted baby blankets into this empty space. I cover up every inch of the crystal until I am looking down at a nest of baby blankets with a fairly large hole in the middle. I fill this hole with small objects such as framed photos, an evening bag, and a little keepsake box containing my Daddy's high school and Masonic rings, and my nursing pin. I then wrap each of these small objects with an article of clothing before putting them inside the cooler. Only when the box is completely full do I tape it shut.

Item 7: Holiday Ornaments
Number seven is sentimental holiday ornaments, a great many of which were handmade by family members. Some were hand-beaded by a deceased aunt who gave them to me as a wedding present. Some were made by my children. There are even tiny framed ornaments with photos of all my family members, close friends, pets, etc. After the holiday season I store these in a special box which is then placed in a small leather suitcase under my bed. This suitcase is something I think my husband spent way too much money on. Because it is so valuable I will not let him take it on an airplane trip because it could be torn

up. So the suitcase is a perfect container to hold my holiday ornaments in evacuations. I have worried that if I put this small box of ornaments up on a shelf it might be hard to find in a crisis, but the suitcase was easily accessible and conveniently located for quick transport. The only problem was once again there was space left over. By now you know how much I hate that. So I decided to store two large lovely family table cloths that had been passed down to me in this suitcase. I only use these tablecloths during the holidays, so it made sense to store them together. So for number seven I just pull this suitcase out from under the bed.

Item 8: Statues and Item 9: Tapestries
Number eight is a pair of very fragile statues. By far these are the most difficult items on my list to pack. One statue is a knight holding a flag and the other is a woman with a falcon on her arm. In other words, there are lots of small fragile pieces which need to be protected when transported. I struggled with a packing solution for these items for a long time. One day I realized that I had two statues and two long tapestries to be evacuated and wondered if I could combine the two. Well, yes, it actually worked well. My tapestries are 86" long and 26" wide. The statues are 20" tall. I took the tapestries down and folded each one in half, making them 43" long. I turned the tapestry work inward for protection. Next I took a bath sheet and laid it down on the folded tapestry. I carefully wrapped a long shawl around the statue, tucking the soft fabric around all the intricate detailed work for padding. If a space was too small for the scarf material I would grab handkerchiefs, gloves, or any other small linen pieces and continue stuffing and padding. After my statues were completely cocooned in soft fabric items (from my home) I laid them on their sides and folded the towel and tapestry completely around each. The bundle was now ready to be taped together, slid into a garbage bag, and labeled.

The Wine and Chocolate Evacuation Plan

Item 10: Wedding Painting

The final item to be packed is an oil painting of me which I gave to my husband as a wedding gift. I love it because it shows how small my waist once was. As my body continues to expand with the years I am determined to keep visual evidence of how it once was. So I pack it very carefully. I pull my bedspread off my bed; take the painting off the wall; lay it in the center of the bed; and spread a soft quilt of great grandmother's over the canvas. Then I take the pillow cases off my pillows and place them down on top of the quilt for even more padding. Finally, I fold everything remaining on the bed (the top and bottom sheets and a blanket) from all four directions over to wrap the painting. Then the bundle goes into a lawn-sized garbage bag, is labeled and now ready for evacuation.

Finally I have all of my top 10 evacuation items packaged and ready to go in the car. Let us just pause here and tally up how many bonus items I will take with me by using unorthodox (but highly practical) packing material. I want to do this because the woman who made the comment, "I have been packing all my life. Why should I learn your system?" had a follow up question. After I explained my idea of using clothing and linens to pack, she said, "How much of a difference could that really make?" Then she walked away and out of my life before I could answer. Well I might not have been able to answer her but I have listed the results from a trial packing I did below. (The first reader to find the mean lady and make her read my results should indulge herself with a box of gourmet chocolate truffles).

Normal Packing	Evacuation Packing
1. Wadded up newspaper	1. Leather suitcase
2. Torn Tissue Paper	2. Purse
3. Packing Boxes	3. Shoes
	4. Evening Bag
	5. 3 Pair of underwear
	6. Yoga Outfit
	7. Sports Bra
	8. Casual Pants & Top
	9. 7 Small Framed Photos
	10. Faberge Styled Clock
	11. 2 Family Tablecloths
	12. 2 Elaborate Table Linens
	13. 6 Shawls
	14. Pair of Gloves
	15. 2 Monogrammed Bath Sheets
	16. 4 Washcloths (matching)
	17. 4 Scarves
	18. 2 Compacts
	19. King-sized Sheet Set
	20. Hand-Knitted Baby Blankets
	21. Throw from my bed

Clearly the right side wins.

Now it is time for a quick review. You have your family and pets prepared and ready to get in the car and leave. You have gathered all your important papers and packed the top ten evacuation items. Everything is stored in your car. Now if you have not already packed your clothing it is time to begin.

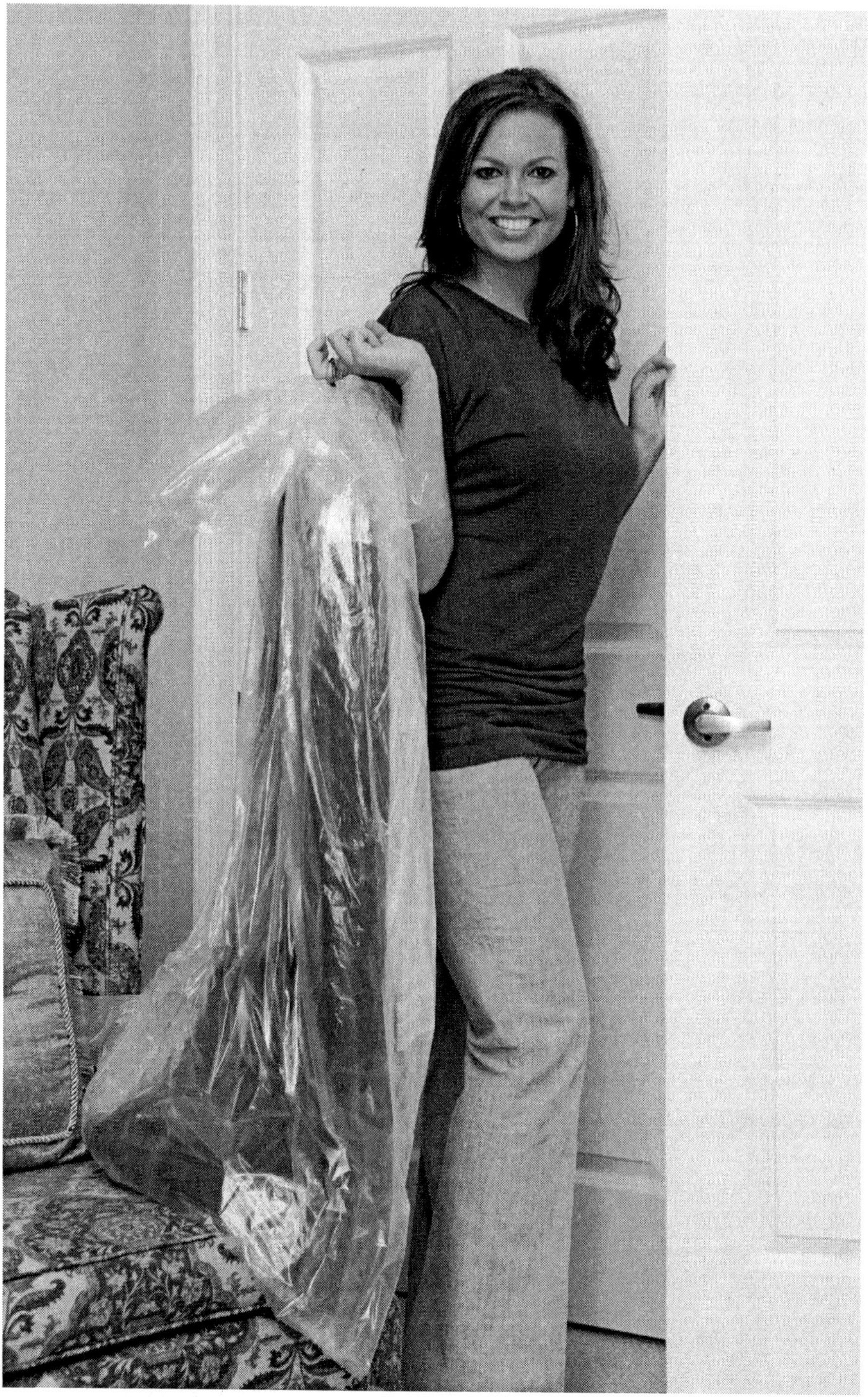

CHAPTER 8
CLOTHING

I think you are crazy to tell people to pack a business suit when evacuating!

A woman once told me, "I think you are crazy to tell people to pack a business suit when evacuating." Perhaps it sounds like I am crazy but if you will only hear me out you might change your mind. If at the end of this section you still believe I am crazy you are allowed to have a chocolate milk shake with whipped cream. I will absorb all of the calories into my body for you. If on the other hand you admit that my "sweet sixteen" of evacuation clothes packing has some merit, we will split the milk shake calories. Where are you ever going to find a better deal?

The mistake most people make in their evacuation packing is taking only a few outfits for their immediate circumstances. After hurricane Katrina most of the people I had direct contact with evacuated from southern Mississippi. I didn't meet one person who had left with more than one or two changes of very casual clothing. All of these people lost everything that they had left behind. I had every person I could think of giving or even mailing me their extra clothing to distribute among these families. It was after trying to help them that I decided that everyone who evacuates should try to take a skeleton clothing wardrobe with them.

The Wine and Chocolate Evacuation Plan

Before selecting your clothes ask yourself, "When I am under stress do I become unable to eat a thing or do I eat everything in sight?" You need to be honest because no one wants to evacuate with clothes which will not fit. You should pick clothing which will accommodate a heavier or lighter weight fluctuation as appropriate.

When you pack your clothes to leave, include a wardrobe from which you can later build. Start with a basic black suit, if you have one. I think all women need a basic dark suit. Ideally this suit would have three separate pieces: a jacket, skirt and pants. If you are older get a conservative style; if young choose a suit with a trendier style. I have a black knit suit with pants, skirt and jacket and two coordinating tops. One top is formal and the other is a plain sleeveless top. This suit packs without wrinkling, forgives my weight shifts and is of classic design. Since I try to pack in complete groups, the minute I take this out of my closet, I grab black pumps and a purse to wear with it. I keep all of these things hung together in my closet. If I only managed to take these seven items of clothing with me, I would have a good and versatile foundation from which to build a new wardrobe.

I have difficulty convincing some people to pack a business suit or formal outfit when evacuating. They are thinking you do not need nice clothing for flight and survival. They are right; you do not need these things for your evacuation. What they have not thought of is what you need afterwards. What happens if you are one of the unlucky ones who lose home and possessions? Your life will go on and you will have to eventually show up for a job suitably dressed. You could very possibly have business meetings with lawyers, bankers or insurance agents related to the disaster. People die during disasters. What if you have to attend a friend, neighbor or family member's funeral? You will need to dress in a presentable manner just when you can least afford the money, time or effort to look presentable. These seven basic items of clothing will not be perfect for all situations.

However, most women know how far you can stretch your wardrobe with a pair of black pants, or skirt and a variety of tops.

The next thing to pack is jeans. At least one pair, but two pair is better. After black pants, jeans are the most versatile piece of clothing in your closet. You can dress them up with high heels and a slinky top and go out; and next day put on the same pair turned up at the hem with a comfy t-shirt to do your housework. My five year old granddaughter wears jeans and looks adorable and so does my seventy-five year old mother. Basically everyone of any age can wear jeans almost everywhere which is good because we are now spending a fortune on them. In order to get the most use from them add three more t-shirts, two regular shirts, dressy-casual shoes and a purse which all will go with the jeans. You will need at least two more casual outfits. These outfits should be what you are most comfortable wearing. You could choose slacks, capris, or shorts. Be sure to pack casual shoes and a purse to match.

Get a lightweight coat or jacket even if it is summertime and 102 degrees because you never know with certainty where you will end up. Perhaps disaster moves in faster than anticipated and you end up in a shelter. The shelter might very well still have an emergency power source and be cool inside. More importantly it could be out of blankets by the time you get there. Remember how chilled you feel after getting wet? Remember how deeply cold you became after going through a shock? Or you may need the coat to shield your face from emergency lighting and get some sleep. You could use a coat as a makeshift blanket to cuddle your children and calm them down. If you live in "fire country" you could use a coat to shield yourself from falling ashes and flying sparks. There are so many good reasons to have a coat, so take one with you.

Finish off your packing with these items: a bathing suit, bathing suit cover-up and flip-flops. You do not need to be traumatized by bathing suit shopping following a natural disaster. It is

The Wine and Chocolate Evacuation Plan

also important to include a pair of pajamas, your underwear, and a sports outfit if you play tennis, do yoga, etc. The very last item to take is a ball cap. You do not want to know how bad your hair is going to look before it is all over.

The Sweet Sixteen of Evacuation Packing
1. Basic dark suit
2. Tops which coordinate with dark suit
3. Dressy black shoes & purse
4. Blue jeans
5. T-shirts (3)
6. Dressy tops which would go with blue jeans (2)
7. Dressy/nice casual shoes & purse which can be worn with the blue jeans
8. Casual outfits (2)
9. Casual shoes & purse to go with above outfit
10. Lightweight coat or jacket
11. Bathing suit
12. Pajamas
13. Underwear
14. Complete sports outfit (tennis, yoga, etc.)
15. Ball cap
16. One clothing item you cannot stand to leave behind.

Place your hanging clothes on the hangers faced in the same direction and secure with a bread or trash tie. Next, take a clear dry cleaner's bag, place your clothes in the bag and tie. Then take another dry cleaner's bag and put it on from the bottom upwards. When you have the second bag in place, tie it around the hanger to seal up the whole bundle. (The reason to do this is because once in the rush of leaving my black pants fell off the hanger while being carried to the car without me noticing it. Needless to say, my perfect evacuation wardrobe fell apart without any pants to wear.)

Chapter 8: Clothing 67

If you prefer a suitcase just take the things off the hangers, fold them, and place them in the case. Better yet, just leave them on the hangers and fold them in half on one side of the suitcase. This method is faster to pack and unpack. After you have put in all the hanging items, gather the rest of the listed wardrobe items and put them in the suitcase.

Of course, if there is any extra space left in your suitcase fill it with other items. It is easy, just keep adding clothes. If you are actually in an evacuation do not think too long and hard. What you do not want to do is stand in front of the mirror trying to figure out which white shirt you really look best in. This is not a date or party night! Just fold them up and stick them in the suitcase. You need to continue this procedure until it is full. Now take your suitcase out to the car.

Congratulations! Should the worst happen you have enough clothing to last for quite some time without worrying. Maybe a generous friend or even a stranger will take your family in. Certainly you would not want to look like the homeless refugee you really are.

Do you still think leaving with a couple of casual outfits is a good idea? I know you want the milkshake without any calories but you must be honest. I assume you are going to do the right thing and admit that I am correct. It is still a good deal because you are going to get a milkshake with only half the normal amount of calories.

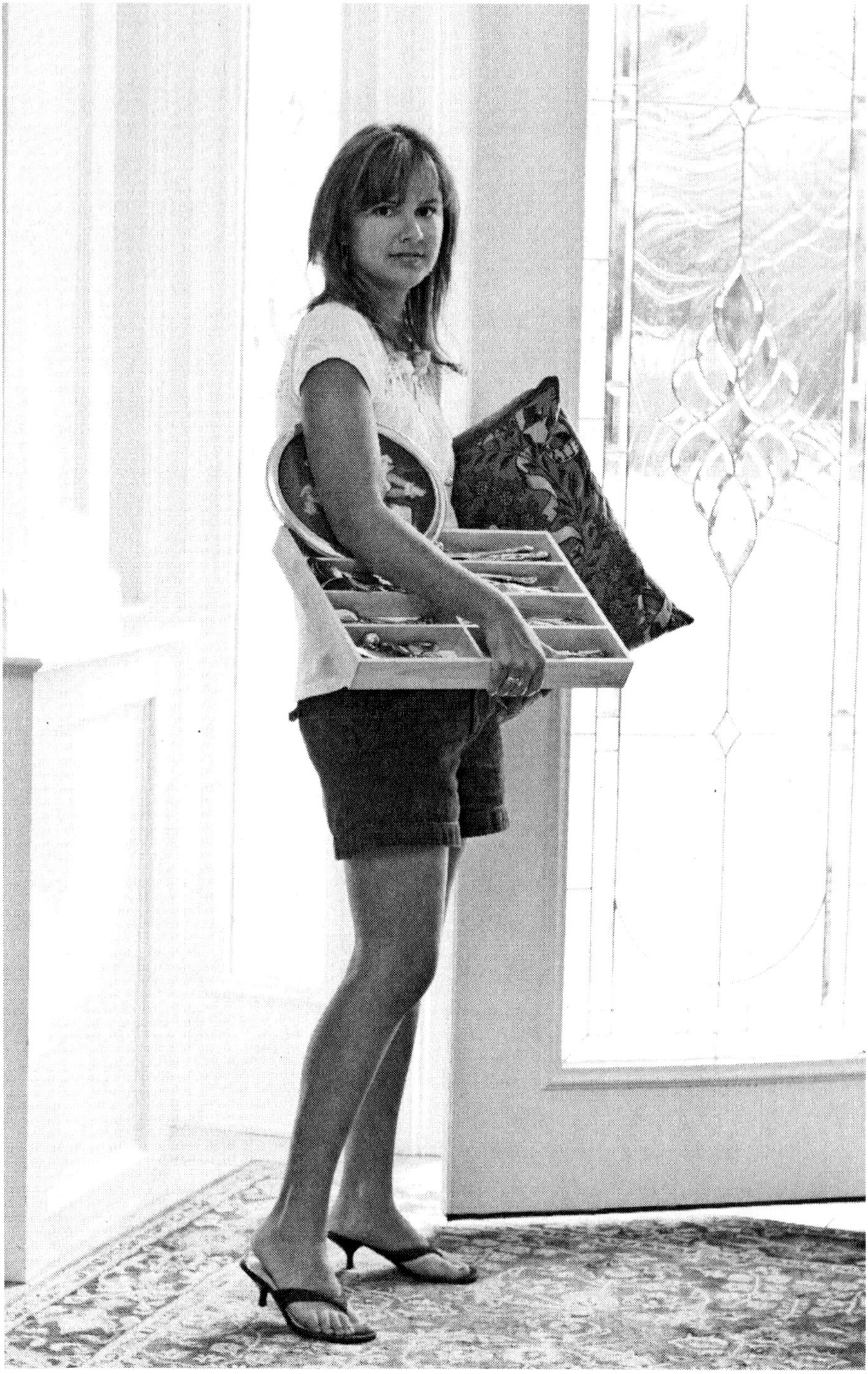

CHAPTER 9
PACKING LIMITS

How will I know when I have packed enough?

This is an easy answer for me because I only stop when there is no more room left in the cars. I always say it is better to take too much rather than not enough. I have met too many people who have lost everything in disasters. My interactions with them have taught me to pack on the side of caution. I think it is a shame to leave an evacuation area with empty space in the car. I believe you should take everything possible if the threat headed towards you is a major one.

When you put the last of the items from the above lists in the car take a good look at the unoccupied space. Do you have room to put more things? If you do, and you have time, keep packing. This is why it is good to have a second list of ten items. If you had trouble filling out the first ten, you will really struggle with this one, so I will give you some suggestions.

1. Flatware. If it is in a tray take the whole tray out, wrap it in a garbage bag, and label.

2. Pillows. Who does not sleep better with their own pillow? What about those decorative pillows you spent a fortune on?

The Wine and Chocolate Evacuation Plan

Pillows are great because they will smash into all kinds of weird shapes to fit the spaces left in your car.

3. Framed Photos. Any framed photo of someone you care enough about to display in your home should be taken. Grab some evacuation approved packing material and fill up your purses with frames.

4. Important Books. You might want to take books such as baby books, school text books, or religious books.

5. Small electronics. Any that will not take up much room (Camera, Video Camera, MP3 player, Kid's game system and games).

All of the above items are fairly small and would probably fit in small empty spaces left in the car. If you had to go out and buy the things again the cost would quickly add up. A couple of the things (baby books or special framed photos) you could not buy at any price but would miss a great deal. I advise you to just keep packing until your transport space is full. Remember to tell yourself this is only a drill, and you fully expect to return everything to its place after the storm, fire, or flood is gone. There is always a brief moment of peace when you have your car completely filled and ready to go. However this bliss is brief because you will then start thinking about all the things still in your home. At this time you will probably be like the lady who asked me ....

Chapter 9: Packing Limits

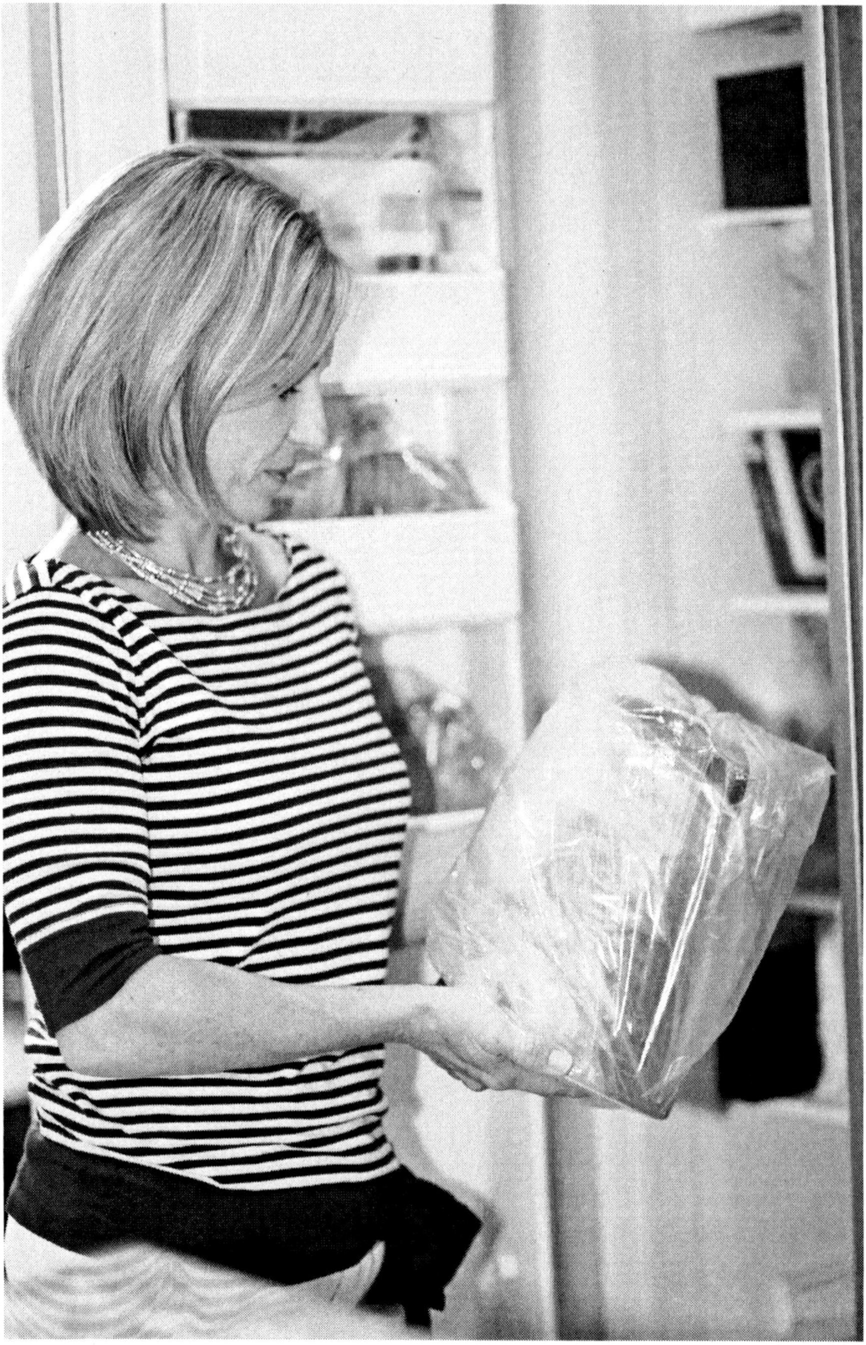

CHAPTER 10
SECURING THE POSSESSIONS LEFT BEHIND

Is there anything I can do to help protect what I leave behind?

Yes there is a great deal which can be done to give the belongings you leave behind a better chance of surviving. There will be precious things left in your home which you simply will not be able to evacuate. You need to do what you can to give them a better chance of survival. How are you going to do this? Once again, the critical point is to plan before the actual evacuation, and identify what is most important for you to protect. How will you identify what is most important for you to protect? You will need to go on a household wine walkabout.

The goal of a household wine walkabout is to identify and record which items have the greatest financial and/or emotional value to you but must be left behind. Example; I try to secure large china pieces such as soup tureens and cherished books. The supplies necessary for your walkabout are a glass of wine, a pad of paper, and a pencil or pen. Now take your glass of wine, pad, and pencil and go into each room of your home. Sit down and take a moment to look closely at the objects in the room. I bet there will be some items you have forgotten about. (When I do this exercise I notice a small framed photo of two of my great-aunts that I have always loved in a guest bedroom.) As you rec-

The Wine and Chocolate Evacuation Plan

ognize a possession which you would really hate to lose, record it on your notepad. After a complete tour of the house transfer the list from your notepad to the space provided below.

Important Leave behind Possessions

Item   Storage
1._____
2._____
3._____
4._____
5._____
6._____
7._____
8._____
9._____
10._____
11._____
12._____
13._____
14._____
15._____
16._____
17._____
18._____
19._____
20._____

After you know what things you want to protect before evacuating it will be time to learn how to do leave-at-home packing. Simply stated leave-at-home packing is placing the things you are unable to take with you in the safest place available. My favorite place for protecting these left behind belongings is my refrigerator and freezer. Most firefighters I have spoken to have agreed that the most likely item to survive a disaster in an average household is a refrigerator/freezer. Apparently, if these are built-in appliances with a lot of weight the odds of survival go up. Ask yourself;

> 1. What are my strongest household items?
> 2. Are any of these household items air tight?
> 3. Can I store something inside any of these items?

A *refrigerator/freezer* answers all of the above questions with a definite yes.

You need to start with your freezer by cleaning it out. The ice cream and popsicles should be the first to go. There will probably be a power outage and they will just melt anyway. If you have kids give them a big bowl of ice cream. It will keep them busy and quiet for a little while. In fact, give yourself a big bowl of ice cream (hopefully chocolate). You have been working very hard and deserve it. Next you will need to get busy and throw out everything you have been meaning to clear out for months. You know things like that huge block of ice with something edible buried within. If you have not thought about taking along a cooler then now is a good time to prepare one. Place the ice cubes from the ice maker into zip lock bags before putting them in your cooler. The ice baggies will still keep your food cold and when the ice melts you will have extra water for drinking or cleaning. As you continue cleaning out the freezer and refrigerator you can throw some family snacks and beverages into this cooler. Be sure to include treats such as juice boxes, jello cups, chocolate bars and a nice pinot noir.

Once you have your refrigerator/freezer cleaned out you can now begin packing into this empty space. Use the same evacuation packing procedure we used before. Take the item to be wrapped, and then wrap another useful item, such as a dishtowel, a piece of clothing, a sheet, etc. around it, before plac-

The Wine and Chocolate Evacuation Plan

ing it in a plastic bag and labeling. Be sure to load your refrigerator/freezer with the same attention to weight loads you had to consider in packing the trunk of your car. Before you pack the refrigerator/freezer you will need to turn off your ice maker. Actually in my area we are advised to turn off the water main to the entire house. You should call your local water company and learn what the recommendations are for your specific area. Whatever you decide to do about turning off the entire house's water supply please remember to shut off the ice maker. During the power interruptions which often accompany disasters an ice maker can malfunction and flood your home. This can happen anytime, not just during a disaster so it is smart to turn off the ice maker whenever you will be gone. I think it would be awful to dodge the disaster bullet and then come home to a flooded house caused by a malfunctioning ice maker.

After you have packed your refrigerator/freezer just take a few steps over to the dishwasher to continue packing if it is empty. If not, take the dirty dishes out and put them in the sink. You will now load your dishwasher with your best china and crystal. If you do not have china and crystal then load your best dishes or best pots and pans, whatever you value and are close at hand. After the dishwasher is loaded, stop and look. If there is any extra space, get some type of fabric to stuff in with the dishes. I think big beach towels work really well. I simply grab a stack of them and lay them on top. I put them in one by one and try to push the towels in between the china to pad them even more. I always think the more padding and protection there is between dishes the less likely they are to rattle around and break. After you are finished be sure to lock your dishwasher door.

Do you have a *trash compactor*? If so empty it and put in a fresh liner. Now go get a lawn-sized garbage bag, and fill it with fabric items, such as a bedspread, a cover or a bulky winter coat. I personally put two rugs from my bedroom and bath into the bottom of the trash compactor. On top of the rugs I put in towels which coordinate with the rugs. I close the compactor and turn it on. After it finishes I load more towels, washcloths, hand towels and compact again. I repeat until my compactor space is completely full. I admit I was nervous the first time I did this. It just seemed wrong. I am relieved to say it has always worked just fine for me. Basically the trash compactor acts as a large space saver. I never put anything breakable in there. I have been tempted because it would be such a great storage space for awkwardly shaped items. I kept visualizing putting this large awkwardly shaped mantle clock down in there with padding all around it. It would be a perfect solution except for.... well, except for me. In the rush of everything I know I would very likely screw up and hit the on button. Then I would be standing there listening to the destruction of my beautiful mantel clock without being able to do anything. So I cannot trust myself with anything but fabric in the compactor.

Look around, what do you have left that will serve as safe storage in the kitchen? I have a large *warming drawer*. It has been broken for a year and generally I use it as a bread drawer. This broken warming drawer becomes very valuable during my evacuation. It is spacious enough to hold many items which do not fit in a traditionally sized drawer - large decorative items that I prefer not to leave sitting out at the mercy of any strong winds which might decide to invade my house. If you have this appliance you can use your evacuation packing skills to fill it.

Most kitchens these days have both a *microwave* and an *oven*. Every firefighter I have spoken to tells me not to pack anything in a microwave. Something about if anything goes wrong the contents become all crispy. So I do not use it. I also do not like to pack in my oven because my microwave is located directly above it and I worry about the relationship of the microwave to the oven.

Truthfully, it is more than that. I do not like my oven and it does not like me. There have been numerous occasions when it has

The Wine and Chocolate Evacuation Plan

let me down. I have given it simple little tasks to perform – cook a roast, melt the cheese on the toast. Rarely does my oven do its job. It betrays me and gives me a roast that no one (even me) will eat. The traitorous oven presents me with cheese toast that has a black bubble that must be excised before it is eaten.

My oven and I are forced to live in the same house together. Like warring spouses we have found it best to try and ignore each other. I know if I put something valuable in the oven the rouge appliance would ruin it just to spite me. However, the oven fears my husband and generally cooperates with him; so if anything goes into that black pit of doom it will be his. I do not know what type of relationship you have with your oven. You will need to make your own decision about its trustworthiness as a storage space.

Happily all is not lost because I have a built in *wine cooler*. It has lots of lovely space and is very willing to share it with any of my possessions. If you have one you should consider using it as a possible storage area. There is an endless choice of things you could store there. You could secure glass or china objects which are sitting out exposed on cabinet tops. If you select something breakable be sure to "evacuation wrap" the item before putting it inside the cooler. You could also store linens, towels or clothing inside there. I like to stick some of my favorite shoes and purses inside plastic bags and put them in it.

After the kitchen I suggest you use your *washer and dryer* as hidden storage spaces. I have a front loading washer and dryer which are tightly positioned between a sink and a wall. These machines are airtight, have large doors (14" high and 19" wide) to load through, and inside contain an area which is fairly spacious for guarding my treasures. This is a great storage space which people often overlook when evacuating.

I pack my dryer with my books. I love my books. They are my old friends. My maternal grandmother was an avid reader and I credit her for my love of reading. When she died she left me her books and I added these to my own library. If you look through my bookshelves it is like reviewing my life. There are children's books that grandmother read to me. Then there are my girlhood books – The Bobbsey Twins, Nancy Drew, Cherry Ames, etc. I have my college books, my nursing books, and my young married wife and mother books. I have noticed the older I become the more I seem to buy, read, and then pass along a lot of them to others. I want everyone else to enjoy them as much as I have. Still there are some books that I particularly like and I just cannot part with, so I pack the dryer with them. I was pleasantly surprised the first time I did this and saw how many I could get in there. For some strange reason my loading the dryer with books as a hurricane approached has always bothered my husband. I would pass him with an armload of books and he would say, "We cannot take all those books." I would reply, "I know we can't." Then I would open the dryer door and start stuffing the books in. My husband would stop whatever he was doing and stare at me for a moment and then say, "What are you doing?" People always say that when what they should ask is, "Why are you doing that?" I reply as I head for another load of books, "Are you blind? Can't you see I am loading the dryer up with books?" My husband always tries to get the last word in and is compelled to finish with "Brenda you know a lot of people would think you were crazy." Well this is not the type of conversation you want to heat up as storm approaches, so I just continue loading my books in the dryer. Since we have been married over 30 years he knows that he probably cannot change my mind so he eventually goes back to whatever he was doing (good time for him to fill all cars and containers with gasoline). After the dryer is completely loaded it is extremely heavy. The last thing I do is unplug the electricity to the dryer so my books will not go tumbling around by accident. I am sure something you have to leave behind will be a good match for storage in the dryer.

The washing machine will be your next appliance to be packed.

The Wine and Chocolate Evacuation Plan

Maybe you have already decided on the perfect item to go into there. If this is so, good, carry on with the packing. If however you are having a hard time deciding what else you should store perhaps you should consider what I do for my washing machine packing. By the time I get around to packing it I am feeling the pressure to be out of the house and on my way to my evacuation destination. So I need to do something quick which doesn't require a lot of thought. I grab some large lawn bags and head to our clothes closets. I then take a handful of hanging clothes, and as I am walking back to the washing machine, I pull the plastic bag over the clothing. I fold the clothing in half and put the entire bundle inside the washing machine. Then I walk back to the closet and do it again. I am able to put three large bundles of clothing inside. I really love the evacuation packing of my washing machine because it is so easy, quick and mindless. It takes me less than 3 minutes to completely load it (2 minutes 47 seconds). Before I shut the door I take a small box of baking soda, open the lid and carefully set it between the bundles of bagged clothing. I do this to prevent any musty odors the clothes might get from being in an enclosed space. The last time I did this exercise, I evaluated what I had randomly grabbed to stuff in the washing machine. In the 2 minutes and 47 seconds I had managed to stuff in 12 outfits of pants and tops (some dressy and some not), three extra pair of pants and one large bulky hooded jacket. Before you get all excited about the potential storage space in your washer and dryer consider where these appliances are located in your house. Now stop and think about the type of disaster you are dealing with. If your washer and dryer are located in a basement and flooding is your concern, do not use them. If you are threatened by strong winds rather than flooding, the basement washer and dryer would be a good choice.

If you take some time to really look about in your home I am confident you will find other safe storage areas. You must take a tour of your home and identify your own safe storage spaces. There are a few points you want to remember in making your choices. First, you need to look for household items you can put things inside. You want the strongest objects possible. The object needs weight to stay put against wind and water force. It is good to have something as air tight as possible. Fire needs oxygen to burn. Should wind get into a holding object it will blow the contents around--- possibly destroying them. The location of the storage space related to the approaching danger must also be considered. A good general rule is that with strong winds (hurricane, tornado) you want to get as low as possible. If flood waters are approaching do just the opposite and get as high as possible.

I only call it a general rule because there are always natural disaster "special cases". A natural disaster special case is an occurrence where the first assault is followed by an attack from a different and often unexpected direction. Probably the biggest natural disaster "special case" in recent history was hurricane Katrina. So many people and houses were able to survive the hurricane force winds only to be devastated later by flood waters. How is it possible to secure your home from danger which will attack from both above and below? If you should find yourself in that predicament (a house which will probably first have the wind attack, followed by the flood waters) try to secure things in a middle zone. I would still advise taking pictures off the wall and breakables off the shelves. Store these items on the middle shelves of any closet. Try to get everything off the floor and bottom shelves. Elevate the lower level furniture on blocks or supports of some kind, and, try to evacuate everything you can from the home.

What about the wildfires which so frequently destroy large tracks of land and housing? Many houses which catch on fire are saved from total destruction by large amounts of water. It is ironic that the very substance which saves the house also is

The Wine and Chocolate Evacuation Plan

capable of doing a great deal of damage. In this type of situation valuables you cannot take with you should go in the most air tight spaces available. The best choice for the majority of people would be the refrigerator and freezer. Next I would use my washer and dryer. After that I would try to store as many things inside chests and dressers that I possibly could. I would pack tightly and take up all the oxygen space I was able to.

Think about all these possibilities as you tour your house and consider different safe storage spaces. Here is a general list to help you get started in your search.

Closets – Fill your closets up to capacity and close the doors. If your area is prone to flooding determine if the closet is in a favorable location or not, and, if you need to empty the bottom part of the closet. Closets are great places to quickly place all of the loose objects you have displayed in your home. It is better to have things covered up in a closet than exposed to any elements which might get in your house.

Furniture – You can store in dressers, chests, cabinets, etc. The heavier you are able to make the piece of furniture the better. Be sure to think of the location of the piece of furniture before loading it up with your belongings and making it heavier. For example, if a chest is located near a window which could be blown out during strong winds try to move it. If you have concerns about flooding, elevate your vulnerable furniture on blocks before filling it. I have a heavy old oak sideboard in my kitchen area. I like to store things inside it because the doors on it lock. After I have everything stored inside this sideboard it is incredibly heavy. It reassures me that it would take a major force to move it.

Car Trunk – This is a space most people simply forget about. Many families evacuate in one car and leave a second car behind with the trunk empty. Cars are really heavy objects and car trunks are well sealed spaces. In addition, cars left behind are often pulled into garages. I think this is a good safe storage space if you are not facing a fire threat. Fire and gasoline are not good combinations. Even if the garage collapses onto the car from strong winds the contents of the car's trunk have a decent chance of survival.

Swimming Pools – I live in Florida where everyone I know automatically tosses their metal and plastic pool furniture into the swimming pool before a hurricane. So I know this method works well to keep pool and patio furniture from blowing into or away from the house. Down in Miami after hurricane Andrew I was amazed by a delicate glass goblet that was retrieved from the deep end of a swimming pool unbroken. After seeing this I began wondering, "Why can't you put other things down in the water for protection?" Then I thought, "Well maybe you can." So I tried it out and it worked just fine for me.

The pool can be used to protect breakable objects that water would not damage. Before I put these breakables under the water I wrap them up. If it is a large china vase I am wrapping, I use a deflated pool float. These floats are made of heavy plastic and I usually have one around the pool. If the object is a smaller china piece I wrap a dish towel around it and put it in a plastic container. When I take this out to the pool I fill the inside with the pool's water, burp the top under the water and let it sink. The reason I put everything into plastic containers is to help protect them from debris which can fall into the pool.

If you have a vinyl liner pool you should not try to use it as a storage area. There is too great a possibility that one of the stored objects could rip the liner. Pool liners are expensive to replace. My thinking is that I could buy a lot of the items I am putting in the pool for what the replacement cost of a pool liner would be.

The following are just a few examples of other safe storage areas within your house. I would bet if you take the time to really look at your house you would find your own inventive places in which to shelter your leave-behind possessions. If you have

The Wine and Chocolate Evacuation Plan

time during the evacuation process, store everything you can in these identified areas. Be sure and record the item stored and the storage place in your book. No matter which disaster you are facing it really helps to have your belongings consolidated as much as possible. During strong winds, items stowed away in closets, cabinets, etc. have less chance of blowing away or breaking. If the home floods then these items would not be as likely to be washed away. In fires remember that the more airtight the storage space the less energy available to feed the fire. Another advantage of packing things away is that you are able to contain the potential mess, which can be caused by a disaster, to certain concentrated areas rather than throughout the house.

    Now that everything is packed away and secured it is time for you to get on the road toward your evacuation destination. If you have made the decision to turn off the water main and the breaker switch for power do so now. Before leaving walk through your house and close every single door. Whatever natural disaster is coming your way make it work hard for it to rob you of your possessions. Remember how people used to say during strong winds it was safer to open all the windows and let the wind flow through? Well it turns out that is completely wrong. Opening the house up only allows strong destructive winds inside. You need to do just the opposite and seal everything up as completely as possible. By closing your home's interior doors you are putting up barriers which the fire must burn through or the flood and winds must break down.

    Good Job! You are done with the protection of your home and can depart knowing whatever might happen you have done your best. Grab your best wine, chocolate, and a good book as you leave. Once you reach your destination there is going to be some down time. As much as you can, this is the time to try and relax. Pour yourself a glass or two of your fine wine; eat your chocolate; and, lose yourself in a good story. Believe me I know how difficult it is to relax under these circumstances. So if you are going to be up all night you might as well have something to read, something to eat, and a little something to drink.

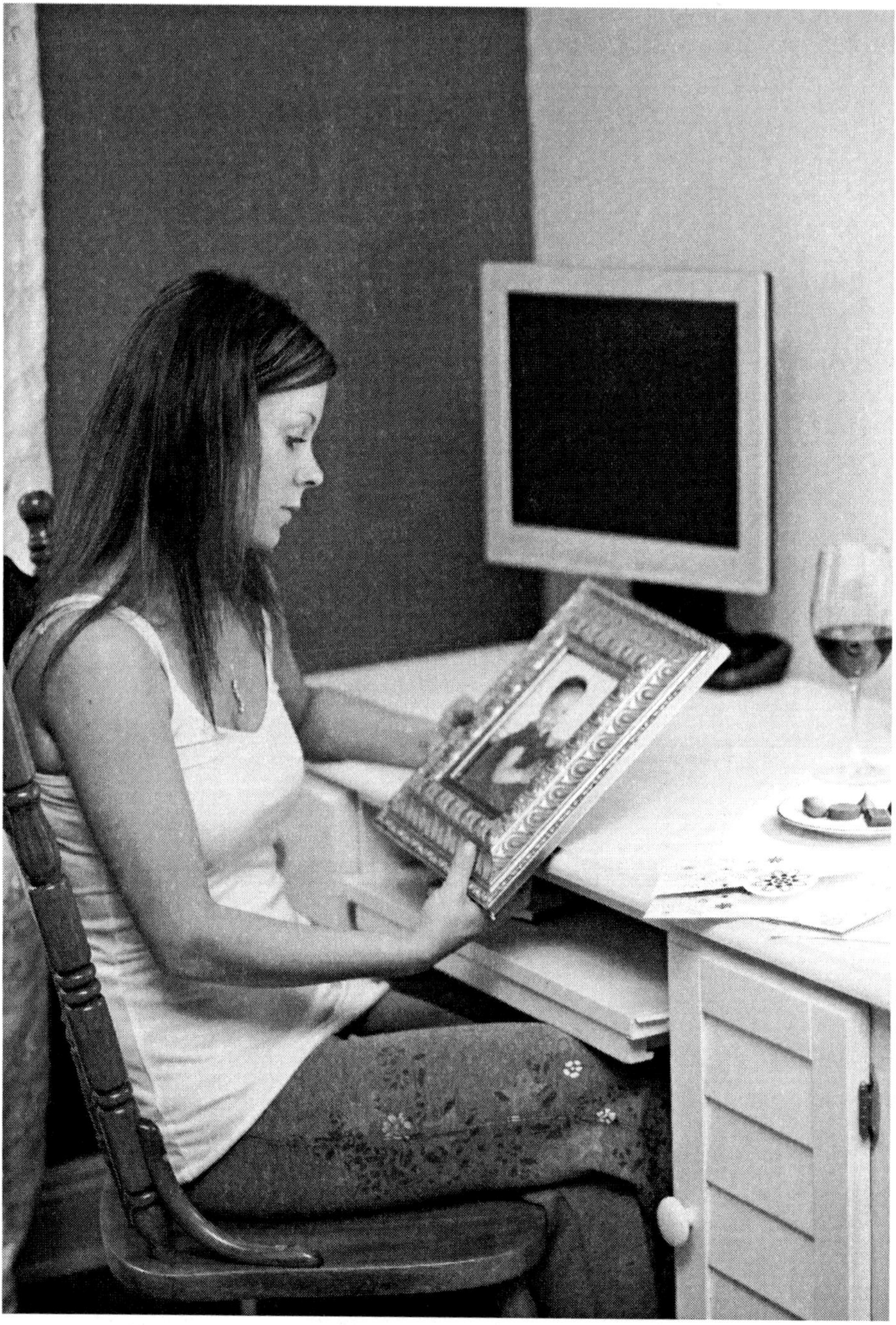

CHAPTER 11
EXTRA CREDIT EVACUATION PREPARATIONS

*What are some fun wine and chocolate activities
to prepare for evacuation?*

I just loved the group of lively women who asked me the above question! I was able to come up with a couple of helpful suggestions for them at the time. I would now like to share my activities with all the other fun loving evacuation planners I have yet to meet.

Activity 1 - Plan a time when you can be left completely alone. You will need to schedule several hours of solitude and gather the following supplies for this activity.

> A copy of *The Wine and Chocolate Evacuation Plan*
> Notepad
> Pen
> A nice glass of wine
> A lovely chocolate dessert

Your instructions are to read the plan while sipping the wine and nibbling the dessert. You should take the time to think about how you would use the book's recommendations for your family. As

The Wine and Chocolate Evacuation Plan

you think of ways to organize your evacuation write them down on the notepad. It is amazing how much you will be able to accomplish if you have a few hours of uninterrupted time to think. If anyone should come by, eye the wine and chocolate, and ask, "What are you doing?" you can truthfully reply with smug satisfaction, "I am planning for the future welfare of my family."

Activity 2 - Once again you will need to schedule some time alone and gather the following supplies.

> Memorable cards, letters, drawings, etc. that you have saved through the years
> Framed photographs from your house
> A small screwdriver
> A glass of wine
> Chocolate candy
> A box of tissues
> Emotionally moving music

First put on the music to establish the proper mood. Then you need to carry all of your other supplies to a table or work surface where you will have lots of room. I like to use my kitchen table. Place all of your framed photos on one side of the table and all of your precious papers on the other side. Be seated in the center with your wine, chocolate, tissues, and a small screwdriver within easy reach.

As you sip your wine and nibble on your chocolate begin to read the cards and letters. Be sure to have your box of tissues nearby! You probably have not looked at some of these things in years and a lot of emotions are bound to be stirred up. After reading each card or letter select which framed photo best corresponds with the card. For example, you might have saved a kindergarten drawing from one of your children.

If you have a framed photograph of the person who did the drawing this would be a good match. Another paper item that a lot of women save is early Valentine's Day cards from significant others. If you have saved something like this and have a framed photograph of yourself and your honey this would be a good match. The Valentine's Day card could also be enclosed in a framed photograph of just yourself or the person who wrote the card.

After you have matched everything up, choose one of your framed photos and the related pile of papers to work with. You should take the framed photograph, turn it over and remove the back of the frame. (This is where the small screwdriver comes in handy.) You will need to remove the extra cardboard which is stuffed in the middle of the frame. The removed cardboard should be replaced with some of notes and cards which relate to this particular framed photograph. The cardboard padding is not something you want to evacuate. Old love letters, birthday cards and your children's drawings are items to take.

Time after time I have seen people show up at shelters with framed photographs clutched in their hands or stuffed in their purses. These people would always say, "I just grabbed the photo as I was running out of the house." I think framed photographs are just instinctively grabbed as people leave during evacuations because they are displayed out in the open.

Even if you never have to evacuate, how cool would it be if a grandchild or a great-grandchild one day discovered a steamy love letter that their grandma had received hidden behind her nice proper photograph. By the time this discovery is made you could be a nursing home resident wearing diapers. Would it not be nice for your descendants to remember what a red hot mama you once were?

The Wine and Chocolate Evacuation Plan

Activity 3 - You need the following supplies for this activity.

A copy of *The Wine and Chocolate Evacuation Plan*
A notepad
Pen
Index cards
A glass of wine
Chocolate treat of your choice

Take all of your supplies to a location near your clothes closet. You should enjoy your wine as you review the sweet sixteen of essential evacuation clothing listed in the book. After you have finished reviewing the list start removing similar items of clothing from your closet. Items should be grouped into separate categories. For example you should have one pile consisting of jeans, one pile of pants, one pile of blouses, etc. Before you begin trying on clothes be honest and acknowledge if your weight goes up or down during stress. You will need to keep this probable weight fluctuation in mind as you start trying on all the clothes. If an item of clothing works and will continue to work after stress related weight shifts that is great! These articles of clothing should be put into a "yes" stack.

After you have tried everything on it is time to review the "yes" stack to determine if you have all the items listed on the sweet sixteen evacuation clothing list. Hopefully you will have everything on the list. If so take out an index card and record all of your wardrobe choices. This completed card will serve as a reference during an evacuation and should be inserted into your book. All selected clothing should then be grouped together in your closet. I like to enclose my entire evacuation wardrobe in a clear plastic bag. I place the shoes and purses I have selected on the floor below the hanging bag. This system decreases my packing time and assists me in staying organized.

If you did not have everything on the list you should take another index card and write down the items needed to complete your evacuation wardrobe. This card will go into your wallet so it is easily accessible when you are out shopping. After you have reestablished order in your closet it is time to reward yourself with a little chocolate treat as you finish your wine. The chances are you are going to have to break down and buy a bigger size of clothing anyway so why not?

Activity 4 - You need the following supplies for this activity.

> The index card listing needed clothing items
> A friend
> A shopping day

It is time to get out the wardrobe shopping list, call a friend, and go shopping. You must ask for your friend's cooperation in assisting you to only shop for the necessary items. Perhaps you need a sensible pair of black pumps but instead you really want to try on the cute glittery high heels. Your friend's job is to help you stick to the list and purchase only the intended items. Once you have obtained the necessary items be sure to stop for a leisurely lunch with your friend. After lunch, if you still have the time, money, and desire for the glittery high heels go back and get them.

Activity 5 - You need the following supplies for this activity.

> A friend
> A nice bottle of wine
> Two wine glasses
> A notepad
> Pen
> Index cards

The Wine and Chocolate Evacuation Plan

Invite a friend over for a wine tour of your house. It is nice to have a friend present to go over evacuation storage plans with you because she will have a new perspective.

She will probably see and think about things you have not. When she arrives you should pour her a glass of wine and explain that you need her aid in identifying secure storage areas within your home. Explain to this friend that a secure storage area has to be strong, as air tight as possible, and be able to hold items. In addition, a safe storage area must be in a favorable location in relation to the approaching danger.

Take your wine, notepad and pen and visit every room in your house. Actually go inside the room and sit down if possible; look around, is there anything in this room you would like to evacuate, but have forgotten about? How much do you have sitting out on display and exposed? Is there a safe storage area located within this room in which to pack the displayed items? As you talk with your friend and consider all the possibilities, you should also be recording your thoughts on the notepad. Label the top of the page with the specific room identification such as Aaron's bedroom, rather than just bedroom. For each room in your house you should identify and record the nearest secure storage area and what you will want to pack from the room

After completing your wine tour of the house it will be time to record everything on index cards. It is also advisable to record some of your notes on the blank pages provided at the back of the book as a backup. You should go back to the kitchen and brew some coffee or tea and bring out the chocolate chip cookies to sustain you while you work. The information you have gathered on each individual room should be transferred onto an individual index card and into your book. The index cards should be stored with your book. These cards will provide you with a room by room, systematic approach to securing your possessions.

Chapter 11: Extra Credit Evacuation Preparations 93

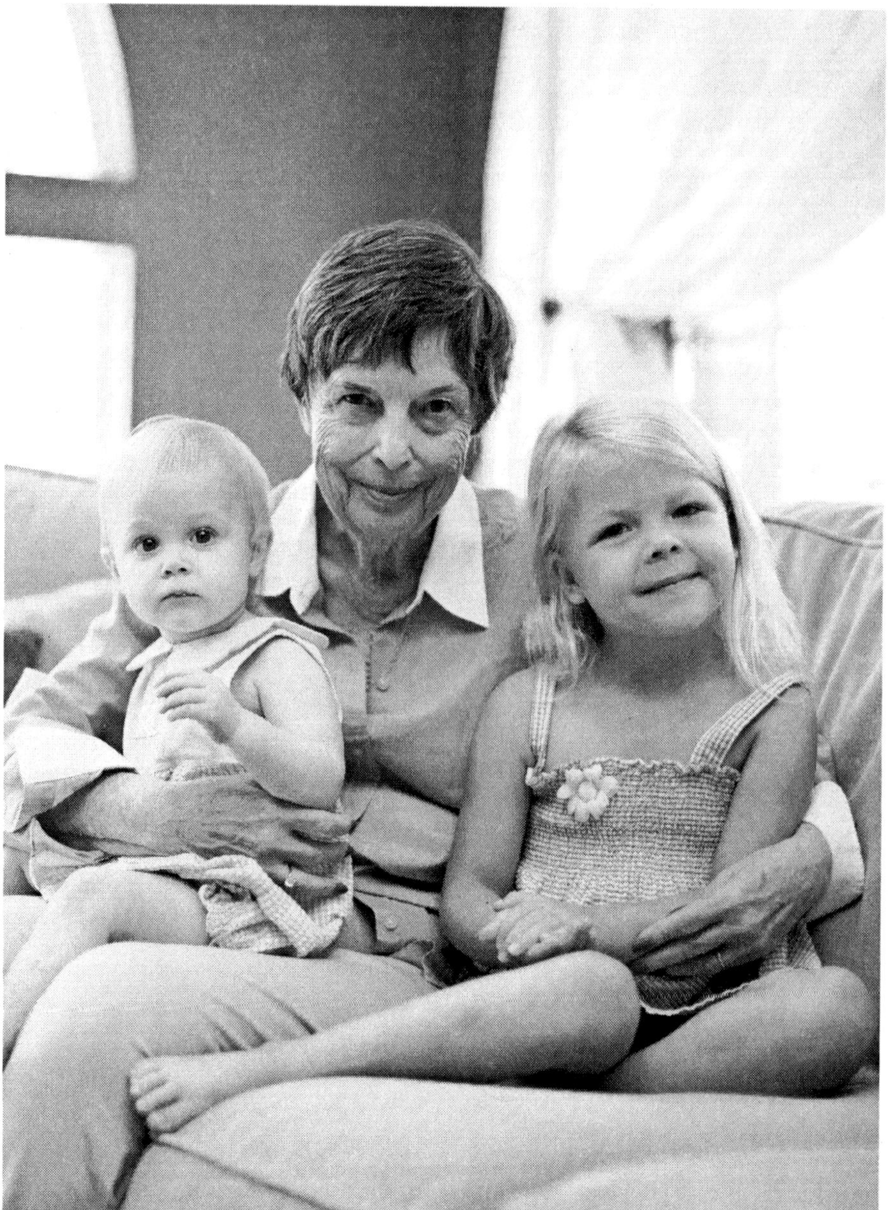

PART II

SPECIAL CONSIDERATIONS

The following section offers some helpful advice related to evacuating with three special populations; children, pets, and the elderly. This section also addresses what to do if you are absent during an evacuation.

The Wine and Chocolate Evacuation Plan

CHAPTER 12
EVACUATING CHILDREN

How can I keep my kids safe during an evacuation?

Know where the children are at all times.

You need to have them close to you. If they are not with you, then make sure they are with a responsible adult. This sounds like something you would just know, right? Well, do not bet on it. Children spend time at friend's and family's homes. While there they could be taken along on a trip to the store, library, dry cleaners, etc. If this were to happen you would not have any knowledge about where your children are when a disaster occurs. My suggestion is to communicate clearly with all the other adults involved. Tell them since there is a possibility of evacuation, your need to know where your children are at all times. If you are the adult who is left with someone else's child find out where that child's parent will be. You do not want to delay your own family's evacuation waiting for a tardy parent to show up and claim their child. Unless it is vital you also do not want to evacuate someone else's child without their parent's knowledge. Everyone should exchange all home and cell phone numbers and keep them available while caring for the other child.

The Wine and Chocolate Evacuation Plan

As children get older there are also a lot of activities they attend without you. They go to school, church, play sports and attend all sorts of lessons. You need to find out what the evacuation plan is at each of these locations. It is important to find the details of the plan which will directly impact your child. For example, if you are asking the school about its evacuation plan and are told "The children will be moved to a safe location within the school" then ask, "where?" Find out specifically to which room or hallway your child will be taken. If the children will be removed from the school ask, "Where will they be taken and by what means and route?"

Even if you have your children at home with you, make sure you know exactly where they are at all times. Tell them they are not allowed to leave the house without your knowledge. No, they cannot go next door to see their best friend. No they cannot play with the dog in the backyard. No, they cannot even play hide & seek within the house. Your kids need to be visible. You want them out in the open where you can scoop them up and leave at a moment's notice. If ever there was a time to encourage them to be couch potatoes in front of a TV or video game, this is it.

During the evacuation dress yourself and the children in bright colored clothing.

It is critical that you be able to see your children and that those children can also see you. All disasters get dark and reduce your visibility in some fashion. (Storm clouds, rain, smoke, etc.) You should put very bright t-shirts and ball caps on yourself and your children.

The importance of dressing this way became apparent to me after a brief meeting I had with a woman in a make-shift medical clinic following hurricane Andrew. She was a Hispanic who spoke broken English. She and her three children had some minor injuries which needed to be cleaned up and dressed properly. What broke my heart was that one of her children had been killed during her family's attempt to leave Miami. She told me they had waited too late to try and get out, and that the weather and road conditions were terrible. Apparently, there were many people crowded into one car. There was a car wreck. The next thing this woman knew everyone had scrambled out of the car. She then found herself out in the rain frantically trying to gather up her children to make sure they were safe. It is hard to see in the rain, but she managed to get three of her children beside her. She could not see her fourth child. She could hear him, but she could not see him and he could not see her. Then something tragic happened. He was hit by something and killed. I think he was hit by another car, but it could have been flying debris (the woman was crying and I hated to stop her to ask for clarification). He died before she got to him. The woman repeated over and over, "He was so close, if I could have just seen him." After I cared for this broken family, they just faded away into the crowded streets. I deeply regret that I could not do more to help them, but there was a long line waiting for treatment. Even though I never saw them again, what this woman told me and the grief on her face still haunts me today. You need to dress yourself and your children in very bright colors. I never want another mother to lose a child in this fashion.

Prepare a small bag full of toys and activities to occupy your child during the evacuation.

If your child has a special stuffed animal or a cherished toy be sure to include it in this bag. Also consider including a book for them to read or for you to read to them. Any activity book which would engage their attention and keep them quiet would be a sensible addition to the child's bag.

The Wine and Chocolate Evacuation Plan

You should place contact information and a family photograph on the child.

If you should become separated from your child there should be a way to be contacted by whoever should find him or her. The contact phone number needs to be physically written on the child's body. There are a couple of different ways to accomplish this. The first method is to simply take a magic marker and write their name and the contact phone number on their back. I learned this from my sister-in-law Ashley who lifted up my young nephews' shirts and wrote her contact information directly on their bodies before we went to an amusement park. I watched her, thinking, "What a good idea." It is important to tell your child that you have written mommy and daddy's phone number on their back. Even young children who are not able to remember their phone number could alert an adult that, "Mommy wrote something on my back."

Unfortunately, as children grow up they start to take exception to this security method. It is very exasperating and it makes no sense! The very same child who writes reminders and friend's phone numbers on her hand in ink, puts stickers all over her body, and begs for a tattoo refuses to allow parental contact numbers on her skin even temporarily. My solution to this is to have a house rule that during an evacuation everyone has to wear extremely bright t-shirts that you provide. Then you must enforce this rule with no exceptions or arguments. Inside the evacuation t-shirts you provide, you will have already written the necessary contact information in indelible ink. Emergency workers and medical personnel are trained to look for contact information in a patient's clothing and possessions.

The younger the children the more important it is to have a labeled family photograph stuck somewhere in their clothing. Separated children need to be reunited with their family and not an opportunistic predator. Things can become very confused during natural disasters, and there are bad people who thrive in this environment. However, a person showing up to claim a child whose face is not in the child's family photo would be treated with great suspicion. This is a safety precaution you want to have in place for your children.

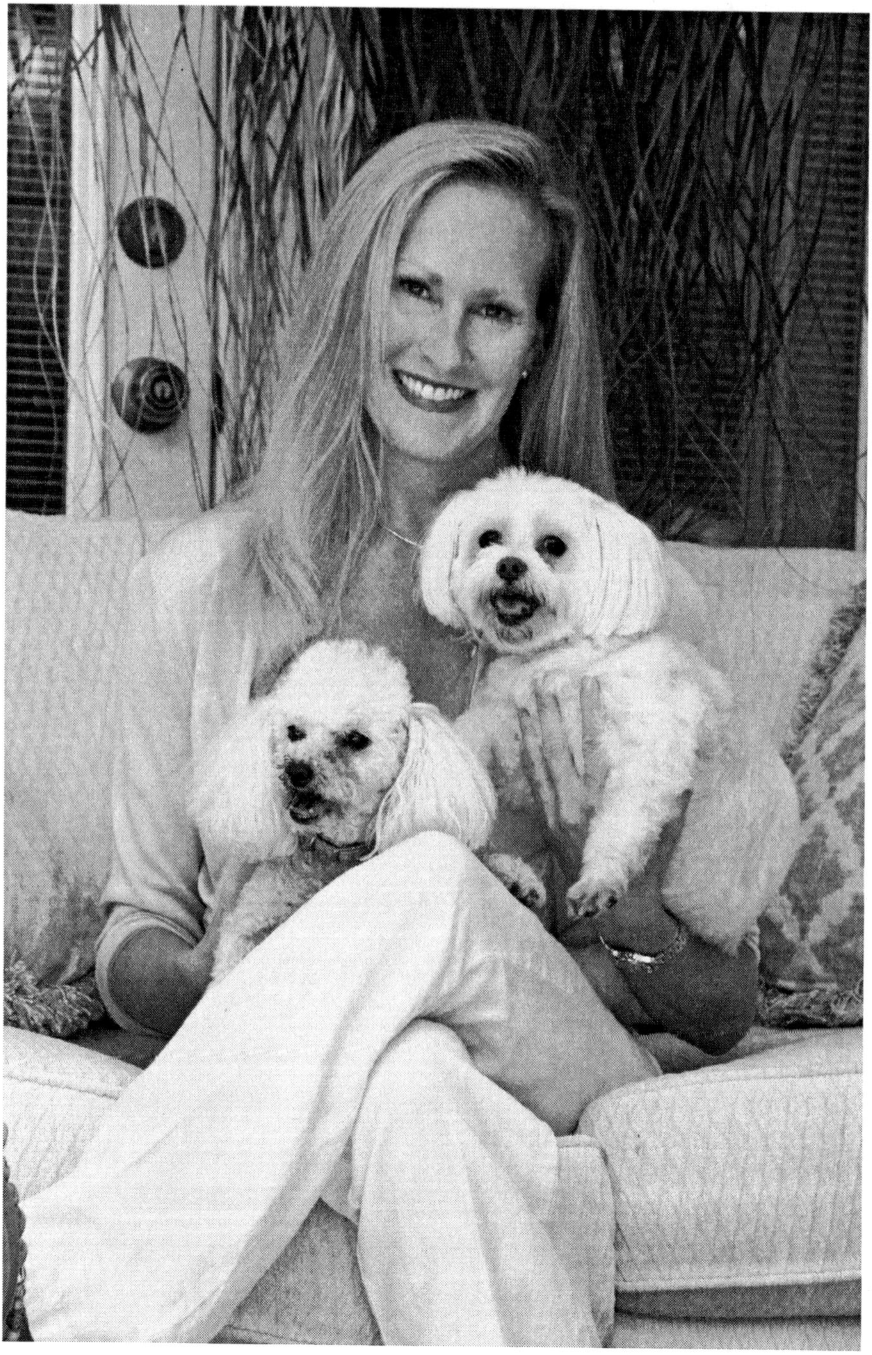

CHAPTER 13
EVACUATING PETS

What should I know about evacuating my pets?

If you are a pet owner you must have an evacuation plan which includes your pets. Removing your pets out of the path of a natural disaster will be the most important thing you do to protect them. Please don't leave your animals behind in an area which you consider unsafe. If the area is too unsafe for you to remain in then it is too unsafe for your animals to remain in.

In many ways it takes more planning to evacuate your pets than to evacuate your children. Before you leave for your evacuation destination, you must confirm that your animals will be allowed to shelter with you. Most public emergency shelters cannot accept pets. Hotels and motels may or may not allow pets to stay. You will need to contact the individual hotel or motel regarding their policies on accepting pets. It is important to ask if the hotel or motel restricts the number of animals accepted, any certain species, or has any weight limitations. Some hotels also require proof of vaccination before allowing an animal to lodge with them. If your evacuation destination is a friend or family member's home you will need to receive their permission before bringing your pets into their home. Not all households welcome animals. If this is the situation at your evacuation destination, you should respect your host's decision and make arrangements to board your pets nearby. It should be easier to find a place to board your animals outside of the impacted area. Remember to pack your pet's proof of vaccination since the boarding facility will require it. Although you may not find this an ideal arrangement, you will have relocated your pets to a safe area and be able to check on them frequently.

You need to keep your pets close to you. As soon as you decide you will be evacuating the area you will need to bring your pets into a contained area where you can easily get to them. If you have outside animals, bring them inside. If you have a cat then put it in a room and shut the door. The last thing you want to do is search the neighborhood for a lost cat when you should be packing up to evacuate. Get the pet carriers out and, depending on the size and temperament of your animal, it may be a good idea to go ahead and put them in it. Dogs should have their harness put on and their leashes on top of the carrier.

Each pet should have the pet owners contact information on their collar or on their transport cage. Each dog and cat to be transported should have a properly fitted collar put on them. If you have a brightly colored collar it will make the animal more visible. Hopefully, you will have a current rabies and ID tag already attached to this collar. If you have these tags but they are not on the collar put them on now. If you do not have any tags, then figure out some way to put a contact cell phone number and name on the collar. (You could attach a small return address label with a cell phone number written in or even a piece of masking tape with the information written on it. Be sure to tape over your make shift ID with clear tape to keep it secure and safe from water damage.)

You should gather the pet's paperwork in a waterproof baggie. Now that you have your pet secured and ready to go, it is time to gather any important paperwork associated with the pet. You will need to get a large zip lock bag and begin placing the pet's paperwork inside. This paperwork may include medical records, ownership papers, vaccination records, licenses, and microchip information. A good current photo of your pet should also go in the bag. If there is no pet photo available and you have a camera, you should take a minute to snap a few pictures. It is best to have photos of your pet taken from the front, left and right side. In case your pet becomes separated from you, these photos will increase your odds of being reunited.

You will need to assemble a pet supply disaster kit for the evacuation. Some of the items which should be included in this pet supply disaster kit are:

1. water and food for at least three days stored in airtight containers
2. a manual can opener if you bring canned pet food
3. food and water bowls
4. a familiar blanket and toy
5. medications
6. kitty litter and box
7. paper towels, gloves, wet wipes, etc. (any supplies necessary to clean up after the pet)
8. a pet bed (if there is enough room to transport it)

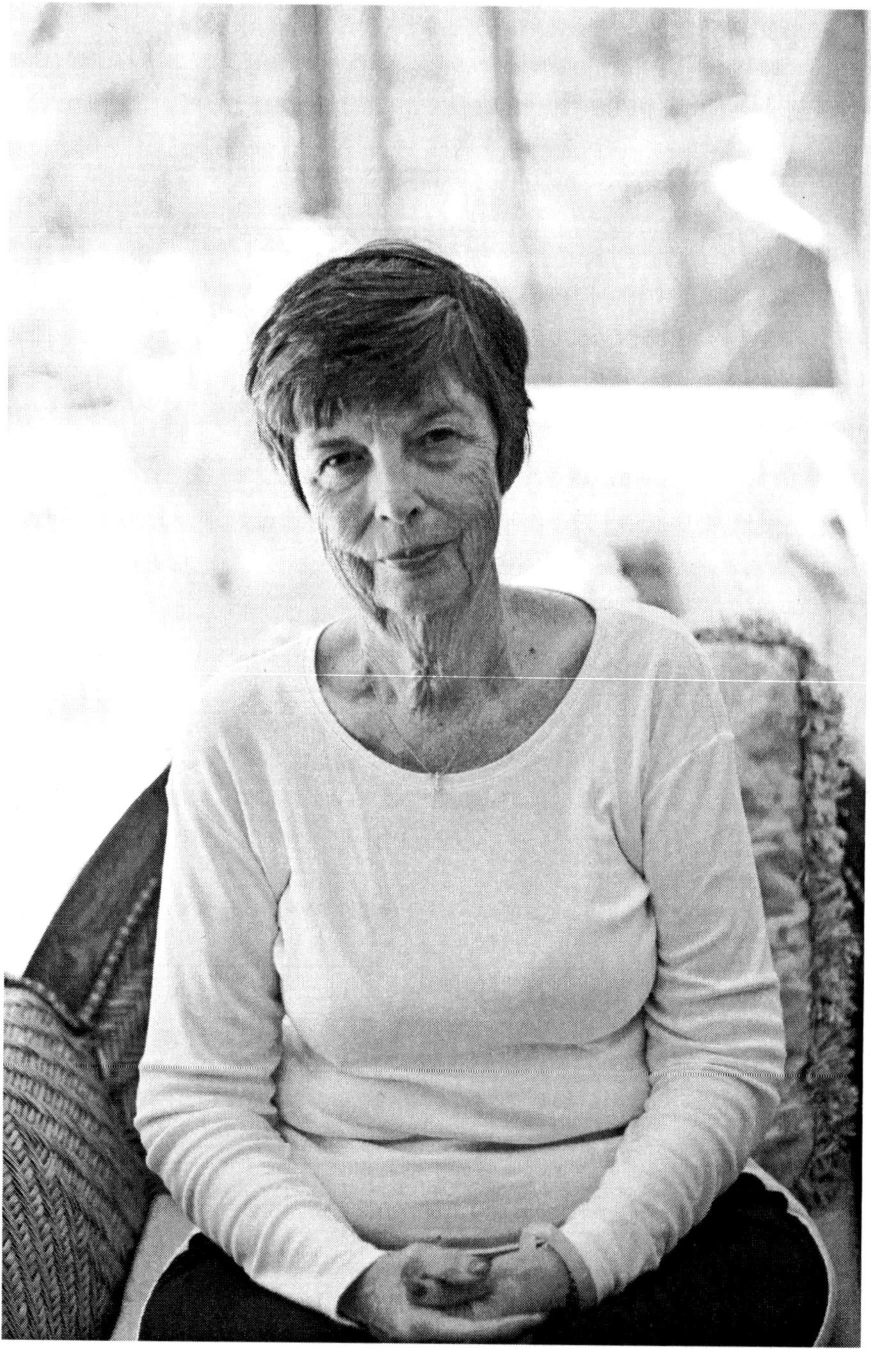

CHAPTER 14
EVACUATING THE ELDERLY

How do I care for elderly family members during evacuations?

When an elderly person is included in your evacuation the process can become very complicated very fast. Usually it will be an elderly parent you are trying to evacuate. Many times the elderly parent will not welcome someone (especially not their child) coming in and taking over their life. You are left with the dilemma of how to quickly take control of the situation while letting your parent appear to be in charge. It is a tricky thing requiring diplomacy and tact. Here are some suggestions which can be helpful.

The elderly person needs to be brought to your home as soon as possible. Many times just getting the elderly out of their home is the biggest hurdle. Their home is familiar and comforting to them and they will not want to leave. Sometimes it helps to say you would just like for the family to be all together during this time of danger. Once you have them at your house it seems easier for them to leave with the rest of the family in an evacuation.

You will need to secure the elderly person's home. When you pick the person up from their home you will need to allow time to do a basic securing of the home. Whichever natural di-

The Wine and Chocolate Evacuation Plan

saster threatens there is always some sort of heavy lifting which needs to be done to prepare for it. Perhaps things should be carried to an upper level due to flooding or bought inside to be out of the path of strong winds. You would be wise to schedule a little extra time to accomplish these tasks.

You must be certain to take the elderly person's medication. The older the person the more likely they are to be on multiple medications. You will need to get a zip lock baggie and put all of the elderly person's medicine inside. Leave the medication in the original prescription bottle. It is wise to also put the phone number of the prescribing physician in this bag in case of a medical emergency.

You must protect the elderly person from dehydration and extreme heat or cold. Elderly people are just more medically fragile than most. You should have some drinking water for each person you are evacuating. A gallon per person per day is what is recommended. It is important to keep them drinking the water and hydrated. Often during and after natural disasters there is an interruption in power. This is a possibility even at the evacuation destination. Although you are not able to do anything about the power outage, you can either cover up or remove clothing to try and keep the body's temperature regulated. An elderly person's health will deteriorate rapidly in the heat or cold.

If necessary, register the elderly person for the special needs shelter in your area as soon as possible. If you are responsible for an elderly person who is unable to travel far because of health issues, you will need to register them for a special needs shelter in your area. The spaces available at these shelters are limited. You have to fill out paperwork and be evaluated for eligibility before you are guaranteed a place.

The local Health Department runs the shelters and should be contacted for specific information related to the registration process. You should be aware that a caretaker has to accompany each person admitted.

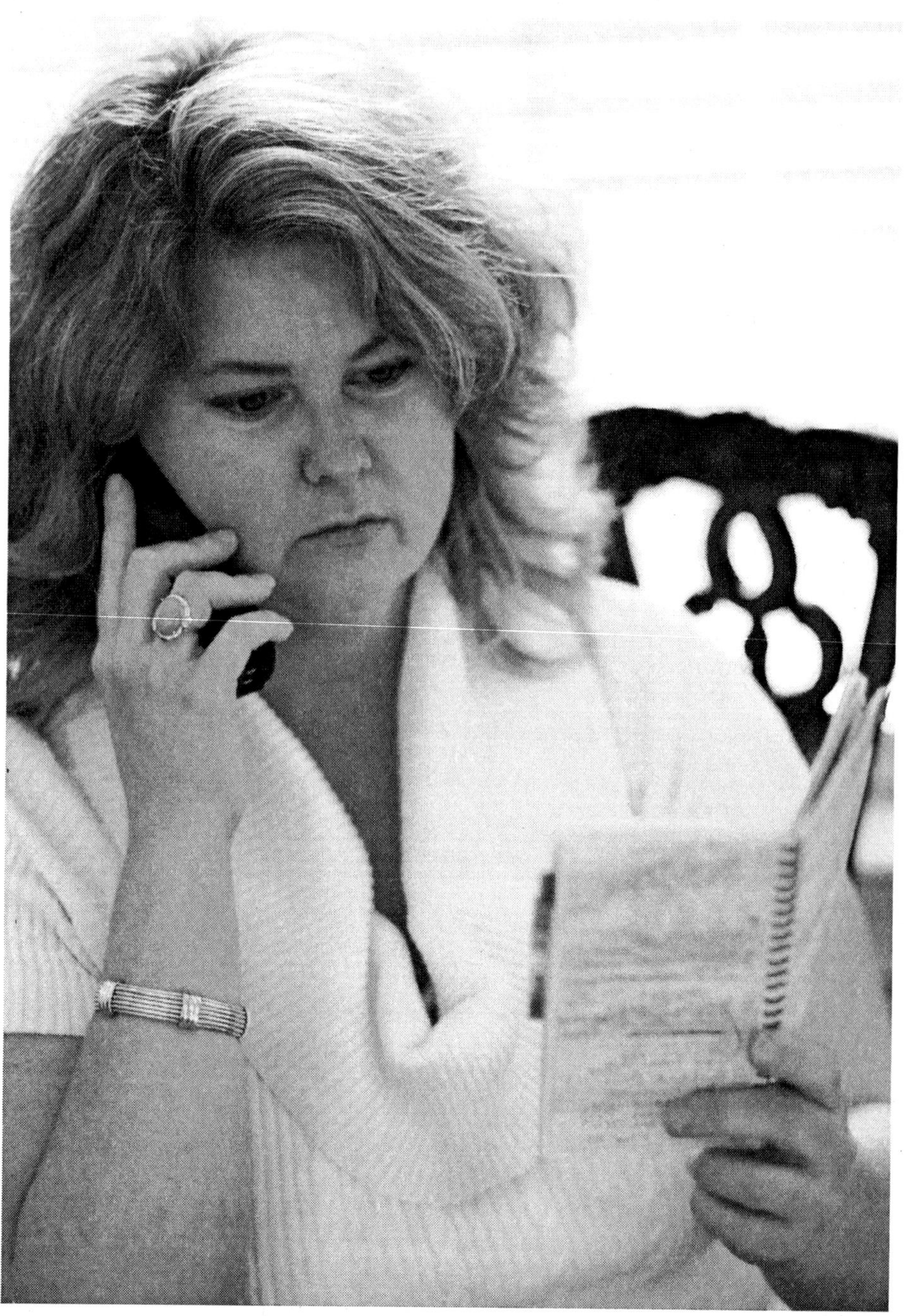

CHAPTER 15
EVACUATING FROM OUT OF TOWN

What will I do if I am not at home during an evacuation?

Perhaps you have read and implemented the preceding evacuation plan. Packing supplies have been purchased and stored. Critical evacuation lists have been compiled. Essential transportation measurements have been taken and recorded. You now smugly consider yourself the queen of evacuation preparedness. I am so proud of you for all of your diligent efforts. Now, what happens if you are out of town when a disaster strikes? My advice is to have a contingency plan in place.

In almost all natural disasters you would not have enough time to travel home, gather your belongings, and safely leave again. This means the only chance you have of anything being evacuated is with the help of someone on site. The list of evacuation items will need to be scaled back to include only your most treasured possessions. Even with someone's cooperation, the key to saving these most cherished items will be adequate preparation. The following steps should help you to get ready.

The Wine and Chocolate Evacuation Plan

Identify and ask a friend or relative if they would be willing to evacuate a few items for you should you be out of town during an evacuation. This is an extremely important decision and you will need to consider it carefully. The most important points to consider when choosing someone are, how much you trust them and how many other responsibilities will they have during an evacuation. The trust determination is something you will probably just immediately know. Most people have at least one person in their life who they feel they can always count on. It is also vital to consider the burden of responsibilities this person will already be attending to in an emergency. You should not consider a neighbor who has three young children, two pets, and a husband who is a firefighter and often away at work. Even if this woman loves you like a sister, she has all she can handle dealing with her own household's evacuation. Also, the person needs to live near enough to your home that the trip would not be a hardship for them.

Once you have made the selection you need to ask the person. It is essential to straightforwardly pose the question and receive a firm answer. Once you have a clear understanding of acceptance from one person you must repeat the whole process with a second friend. The second person will be your back up evacuator in case the first person is unable to help you at the last minute.

Before leaving on a trip consolidate your evacuation items as much as is possible. This should not be a big packing job. Do not expect your friend to carry a great deal out for you. Perhaps a suitcase filled with some of the smaller things on your evacuation list. Remember someone is doing you a great favor by taking time away from their own evacuation plans to come and help. You will be asking them to give up some of their own valuable car space to transport your things to safety.

Have a written list of the items you are requesting to be evacuated and their location posted by your telephone.

Once again, you are asking a friend to do you a great service, so keep it as easy as possible for them. Please don't have them running around your home trying to figure which oil painting you want to go. You need to list the evacuation items and their location on a colored index card and tape it in a prominent place beside your telephone.

Even while traveling be aware of conditions at home. This can be accomplished in a variety of ways. It can be as simple as turning on the weather channel and checking the forecast for your home area. You could call home and chat with your best friend for a few minutes every day.

You should take all of your important contact phone numbers with you when you travel. If you have your contact numbers readily available it will enable you to quickly call your key people and activate the contingency plan.

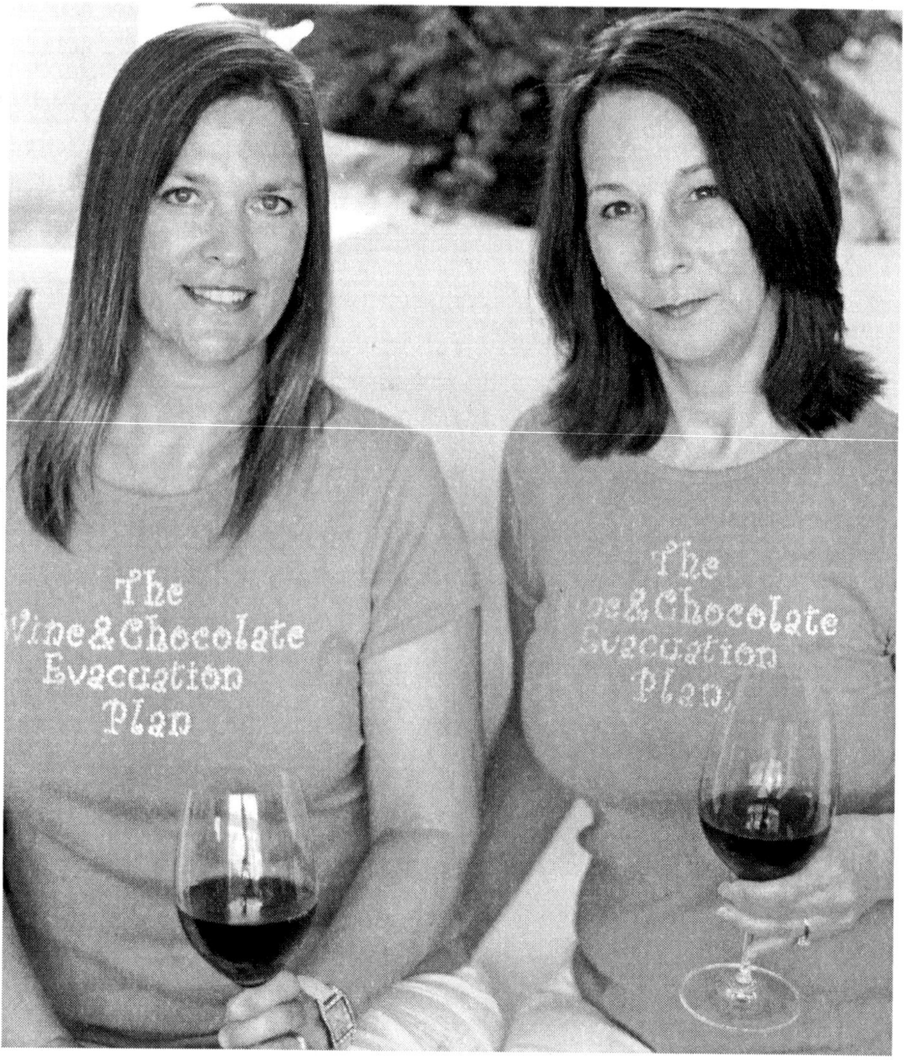
The
ine&Chocolate
Evacuation
Plan

PART III

WINE & CHOCOLATE EVACUATION PARTY

Why Host A Party?

For fun and because we have done all the planning for you.

You will help your friends become better prepared for an evacuation, and everyone will have a good time in the process.

You will definitely be better prepared for evacuation because you will have to read and explain the material to others.

It gives you an excellent altruistic reason to go out and buy wine and chocolate.

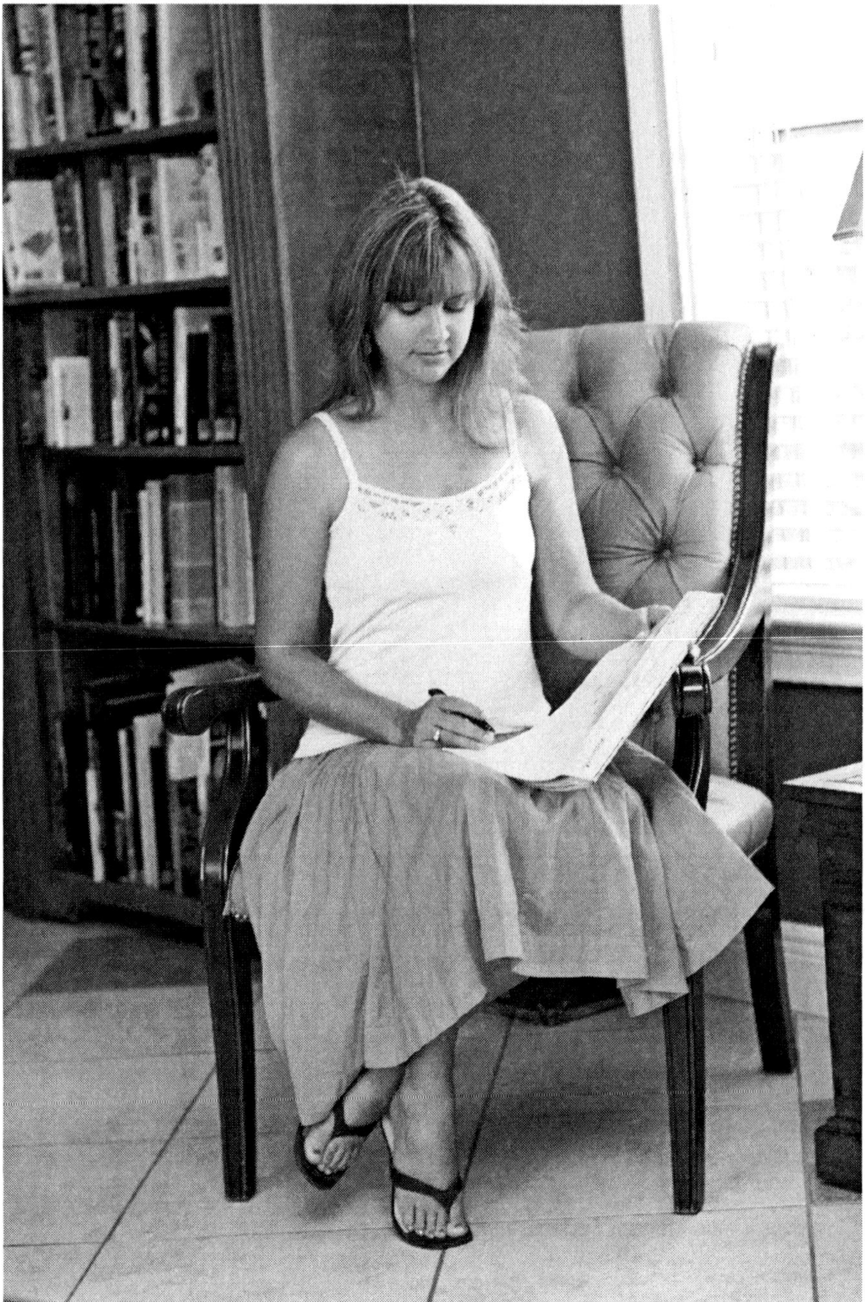

CHAPTER 16
TIMELINE

A step-by-step guide on how to host a wine and chocolate evacuation party.

1. You should get a friend to co-host with you, (because one of you must talk to the guests you both can't be shy people). There are many advantages to hosting with a friend including sharing the cost, pooling the necessary supplies (wine glasses, scissors, flashlights, etc.) and just having a good time together while you plan the party.
2. Read *The Wine and Chocolate Evacuation Plan.*
3. A date for the party should be chosen and the invitations prepared. An outline for the invitations is available for printing from the www.wineandchocolateplan.com web site. (These invitations have been designed to be used in a party activity. They will also be useful to each guest following the party.)
4. Complete all the party preparation activities listed below
5. Go shopping for party and food supplies. A sample menu and a party supply list are included in the party plan.
6. Practice with your 22 steps party cards and poster boards at least once before the party.
7. Have a glass of wine before your guests arrive.
8. Have fun at the party!
9. Clean up the next day.

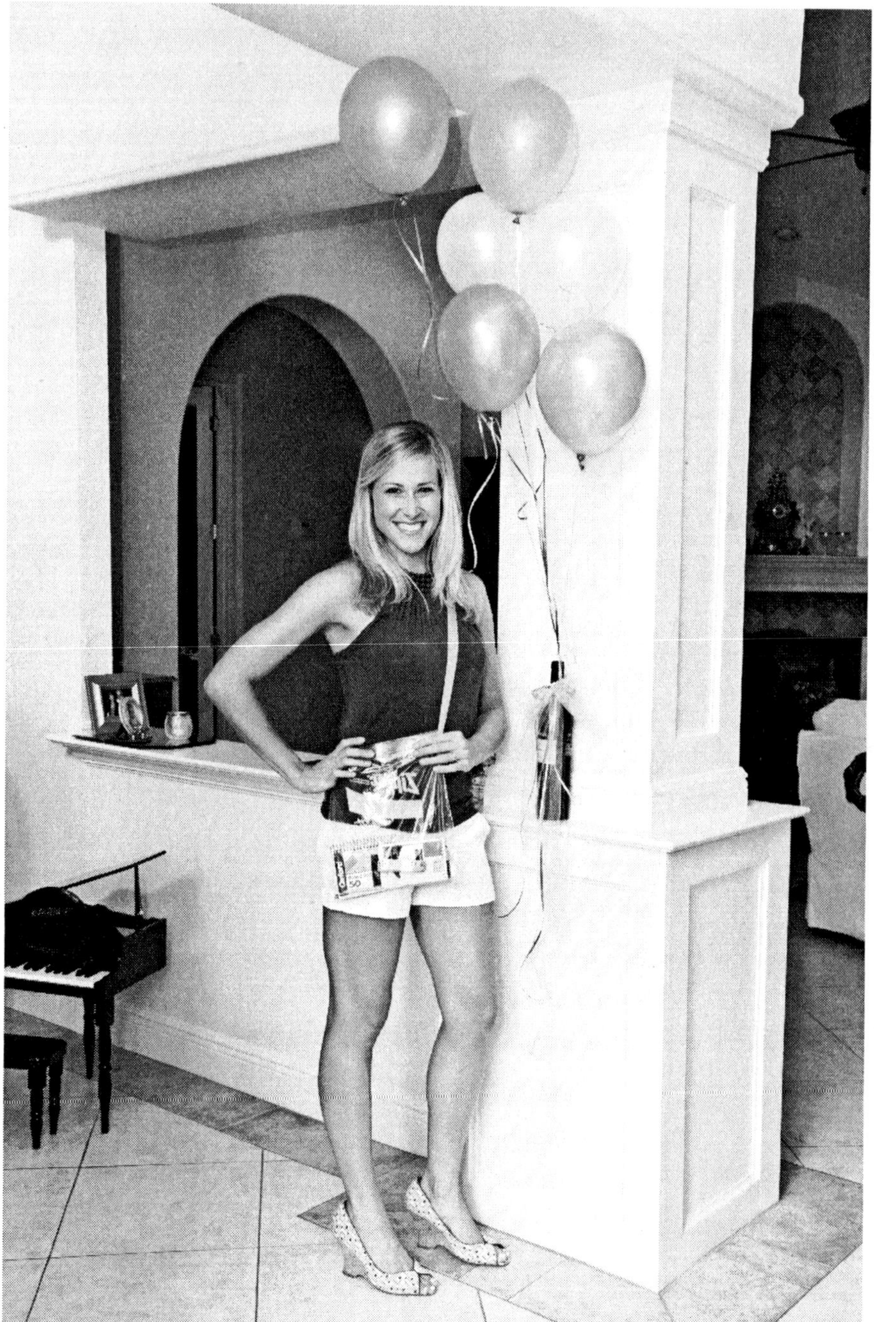

CHAPTER 17
ADVANCE PARTY PREPARATIONS

Everyone, including the hostess, should have fun at the party!

Advance preparations are the way to make sure this happens. During the actual party it is important to devote your time and energy to your guests and the information you wish to share with them. Once you have completed the following advance preparations you will have a step-by-step format to follow during the party. This plan will eliminate the hostess' need to memorize any information. She will have everything written down on cards or posters so all she has to do is read them to her guests.

Step-by-Step Perfect Party Cards

Take a stack of loose index cards. On the first card write down the instructions in step number one from the 22 steps to a perfect party section of this guide. Abbreviate the information. For example the first card could say, greet guests, check invitations, and enter names in drawing for the door prize. Now continue filling out a separate card for each step. These cards will make it easy for you to direct the party.

The Wine and Chocolate Evacuation Plan

Powerful Pink Poster Boards

Get out the bright pink poster boards and your markers. Copy the 8 italicized sections onto the 8 posters. (Feel free to let your inner artist go wild and maybe add some glitter to jazz things up a bit.)

Party Favors

I suggest giving your guests the evacuation essential necklace as a party favor. It is an easy and useful gift. You should buy a whistle on a lanyard for each of your guests. All that is left to do is attach small flashlights of some kind to the lanyards.

Party Packs

To construct your party packs you should start by taking a gallon sized zipper-top plastic bag and cut a small hole at the top of each side of the baggie under the seal. Next make a long handle for each of the party packs. To do this cut a yard and a half of bright pink ribbon, thread a ribbon end through each hole and tie in a secure knot. You should finish by filling the packs with a pen, a pencil, a single ruled 3x5 index card, a flip-topped ruled index card pad, and a tape measure.

Prizes

Wrap the two prizes in some bright pink paper and ribbons. I recommend giving a door prize early in the party. I have structured the party timetable so that serious subject matters are interspersed with fun activities. My suggestion for the door prize is to wrap up a box of space saving travel bags and a luxury chocolate bar. Use bright pink wrapping paper and a big bow with a copy of The Wine and Chocolate Evacuation Plan placed under the ribbon. The grand prize (which should be given at the end of the party) should be a big box of garbage bags, a box of space saver travel bags, and two boxes of zipper-top baggies. It looks good to wrap each box separately in bright pink paper and build a tower of pink with ribbons and a copy of the book at the top. Once you have wrapped this prize, it can do double duty as a party decoration.

Wine Glasses and Wine Charms

Count your wine glasses and wine glass charms to make sure there will be enough for your guests. If you have a co-hostess you will probably be able to combine your wine glasses and have enough for the party. The wine charms can be as simple as tying different colored ribbons on the stems of the wine glasses or as elaborate as creating beaded rings with actual charms attached.

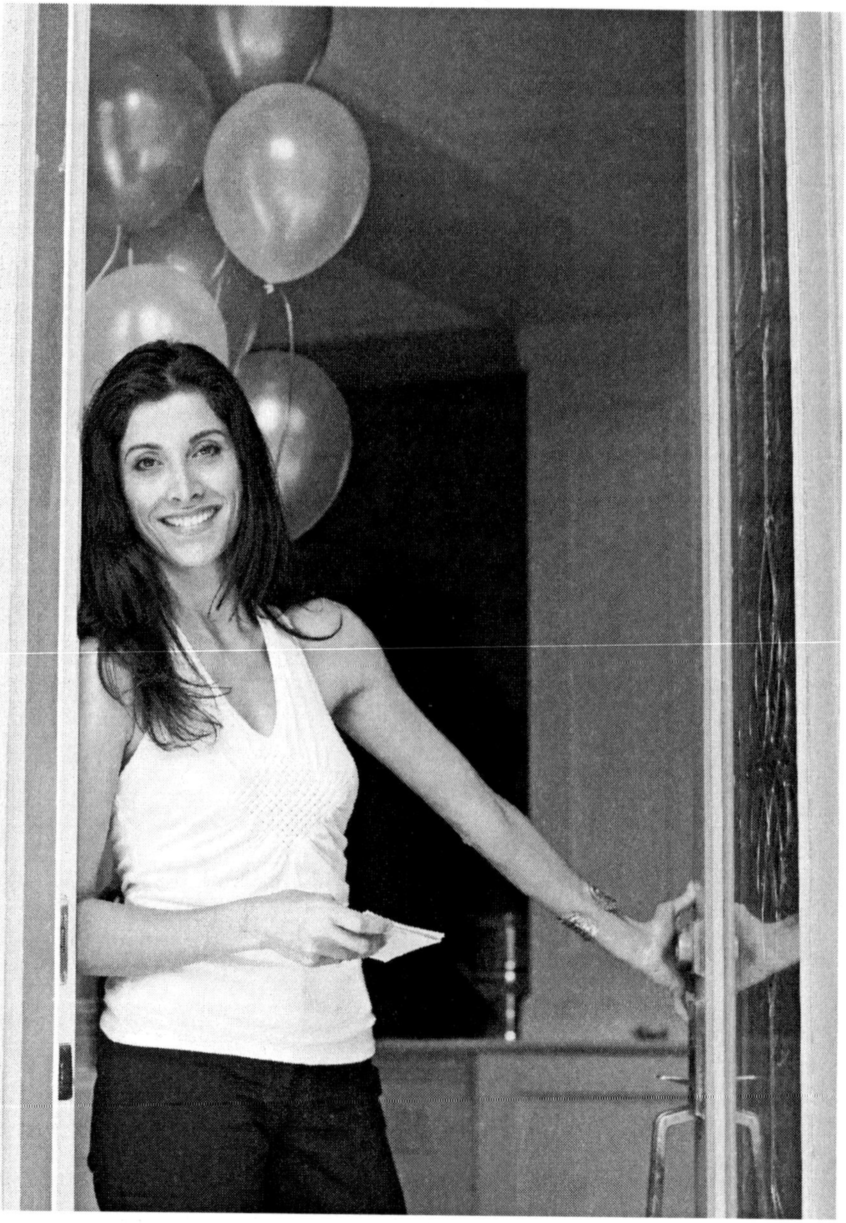

CHAPTER 18
22 STEPS TO A PERFECT PARTY

1. As your guests arrive one hostess should be at the front door to greet them. This hostess should check each guest's invitation to see if the required homeowner's information has been filled in. If so, then write this person's name down and drop it in a bag for the door prize drawing. If the person has not filled in the information or forgotten her invitation then her name is not put into the drawing. Give her a new invitation and remind everyone to hold onto the invitations as they will need them during the party.

2. Place a lanyard with an attached whistle and a small flashlight around each of your guest's neck. Instruct the guests to also attach their car keys to the lanyard. Next hand each guest some play money and ask them to put it in their bra.

3. Direct all guests to a second location where they will be able to pick out an identifying wine charm and receive their first glass of wine. At this location everyone gets to enter their name in the drawing for the grand prize. The second hostess

The Wine and Chocolate Evacuation Plan

should be stationed at this location to pour everyone a glass of wine and offer the chocolate. Please be kind to the people who did not get to be in the first drawing and pour them a generous glass of wine.

4. Everyone should mingle and enjoy the food, wine and chocolate until all the guests have arrived.

5. Once everyone is present direct them into an area where everyone will be able to sit down, drink their wine, and write comfortably.

6. The main speaker should start by thanking everyone for coming and explaining why you decided to host the party. You may simply state: "The purpose of the party is to have a good time and help you leave this evening better prepared for evacuation than when you arrived."

7. It is important to emphasize the most important fact about evacuation. You should write this message on a poster board which can be prepared in advance. You will then read it to your guests.

> You and all living things in your household are the most precious items to be evacuated. Never stay or go back into a dangerous area for anything which doesn't breathe. If you lose everything you possess but are able to save yourself, your family, and your pets then you have been successful.

Posterboard #1

8. Explain the importance of each "evacuation essentials" you have had the guests place on their bodies.

> - *Cash* - Purses can be lost and the technology supporting credit cards can fail but cash from your bra will never let you down.
> - *Small flashlight* - Disasters get dark. During an emergency you need an easily accessible light source to help guide you.
> - *Whistle* - Blowing a whistle is an international distress signal. The sound would attract rescue attention.
> - *Car Keys* - During the confusion of packing for an evacuation car keys can and often are misplaced. You should keep the car keys on your body.

Posterboard #2

9. Pass out the party packs and go over the contents. Contained within the packs you will have a pen, a pencil, a single ruled 3x5 card, a flip-top ruled index card pad, and a tape measure. The party packs are to be worn like a purse across your body leaving your hands free to work.

10. Ask everyone to present their invitations. You will need to have several pairs of scissors available. Everyone will now cut out the homeowner's or renter's policy card from the invitation and put it into their wallet. If you have your copy of The Wine and Chocolate Evacuation Plan it would be wise to record the numbers into the important documents section of the plan. Even if someone has forgotten to bring the information, have them cut out the blank card and put it into their wallet. I know this sounds strange but if someone does

The Wine and Chocolate Evacuation Plan

this much they are more likely to go back and complete the required information. Congratulate everyone on being one step better prepared for an evacuation than when they arrived.

11. Now is the time to draw for the door prize only for those who arrived with their homeowner's or renters' insurance information filled out. Give the winner one practical item related to packing supplies and one "I just need it!" item from the wine and chocolate category. I usually give a box of those space saving travel bags, a luxury chocolate bar, and a copy of The Wine and Chocolate Evacuation Plan.

12. For the next activity ask all guests to take out the single ruled index card and a pencil from their party pack. Have the ladies push their wine glasses to the center of the table noting which wine charm is on their glass. Start a CD with storm sounds in the background. The storm sounds will help create the atmosphere one has think in when a disaster approaches. Say to your guests, "You have already gathered your important papers and arranged for the evacuation of all your family members and pets. There is still some time before you must leave. Please list the ten items most valued items you would most want to leave the house with. You have four minutes."

    Your co-hostess should be timing everything. After 2 minutes turn the lights off, but leave the storm sounds playing. Immediately, everyone will start asking, "What happened to the lights?" Tell them it's a disaster and the power has gone off. Remind them that they have small flashlights on their evacuation necklace. Let them continue fumbling around in the darkness and trying to finish their lists for the next 2 minutes. If they whine tell them this is what really happens in emergency situations.

    When the 4 minutes are up turn the lights back on and let everyone retrieve their wine glass. At this point refresh the guests' wine and pass the chocolate. You should reassure everyone that it was only a practice exercise, a practice card, and the ten selected items do not have to be their final answer. After the darkness and scary sounds your guests will need a few minutes to settle down, review and reflect on their choices.

13. Very few people make the best choices when they are under duress. This is why it is better to make important decisions such as, "What should I evacuate?" when not under stress. Now show your guests poster board #3 and go over it with them. This poster board will read:

> **When selecting your evacuation items consider:**
> *Which items do you consider emotionally irreplaceable?*
> *In the time I have what do I have the capacity to carry out with me?*

Posterboard #3

Take the time to go over each question separately.

Only you are able to determine which items you would grieve over if you lost them. Give this question careful thought and answer from your heart.

To address the second part of the above two questions review poster board #4 with your guests. This poster board will read:

> To determine which possessions I have the capacity to evacuate it is essential for me to know what vehicle I will be leaving in, how much space is in this vehicle, and if I will have to share that space with others.

Posterboard #4

The Wine and Chocolate Evacuation Plan

There are two ways to handle this question. You will be able to decide which scenario will be the best for you, your guests, and the environment in which your party is being held.

The first activity will work best if the party is being held at a house where the guests have parked directly outside of the dwelling. Both the weather and your guests will have to be cooperative. It will require more effort from the guests to do this activity but it will yield the most useful results.

Scenario #1 -- In order to determine how much transport space your guests will have available to them everyone will need to go outside. They should all have their car keys around their necks and their party packs across their bodies. Have your guests follow you outside to your car. Open up the trunk and demonstrate how to measure the space available for storage. The car's trunk measurements and the rear seat measurements should then be recorded on the second page of the flip top index card pad.

Next send them off to measure their own car's space. If someone did not drive to the party they do not get to skip this activity. They are paired up with someone else who has a similar car. The person without a car should measure their partner's car for practice. Then they should label page number two in the flip top pad "car space" and fill in the dimensions at home once they have actually measured their own vehicle.

Scenario #2 -- Should it be raining outside your guests would not want to trudge outside to measure their car's storage space. What if the party is being held in an apartment building and the cars are some distance from the party site? It would not be a good use of the party's time to send people out on a lengthy task.

The best way to demonstrate your point under these circumstances is to provide a visual illustration of a sample car's storage space. You should have the dimensions of two sample car's trunks and rear seat spaces cut out of newspapers and taped together. (I use a sedan and a minivan as the examples.) After you have unfolded the two examples of transport space, you should ask each of your guests to tell you the largest item that they have on their list. Now go to the car which is the closest match to their car and measure to see if this item would fit. Of course you will not have the exact measurements of their car or the item, but you will be able to estimate close enough to know if the transport of any particular item will be a problem.

The goal of these exercises is to have guests select the possessions they most want to take; and then plan for the necessary transport space the evacuated possessions will require.

14. Now share poster board number five with your guests. This poster will contain the survey results of what 100 women said they would evacuate when they were told, "You have already gathered your important papers and arranged for the evacuation of all of your family members and pets. There is still some time before you must leave. Please list the ten items you would most want to evacuate from your house."

| **What 100 Women Would Most Want to Evacuate** |
| (Survey Results In Descending Order) |

1. Photos	6. Personal Keepsakes
2. Clothes	7. Toiletries
3. Jewelry	8. Shoes
4. Food and Water	9. Antiques
5. Computer	10. Original Art and Linens

Posterboard #5

The Wine and Chocolate Evacuation Plan

I have found that knowing what other women have chosen as their evacuation items stimulates a lot of discussion. Some women are prompted to remember items which were not included on their original list. Others disagree with items on the above survey list and will voice their opinions. Most importantly, everyone gets involved and starts thinking about what they really want to include on their personal lists.

15. You should ask everyone to take out their neon flip top pads and turn to the third page. Instruct them to draw a line down the center of the page; label the left hand side of the page "item," and label the right hand side of the page "location"; number the lines from 1-10. Tell everyone to write down their evacuation items on the left hand side of the page and where they are located in their home on the right hand side of the page.

16. After they have recorded all ten of their evacuation items they are instructed to record each identified item on a separate card in their pads. These cards will act as packing labels. During an actual evacuation having these cards written out helps to keep the packing process organized and saves time. If one of the evacuation items is a multiple then the item should be placed on multiple cards. Probably the most common example of this is photos. If someone does not know exactly how many photo albums they have, instruct them to fill out several cards. Maybe they will have to make more labels, but since they have already started it will be a quicker task.

17. Now that your guests have decided what they will take with them it is time to wrap these things up for transport. Show them poster number six which reads:

> In an evacuation everything you take with you, including your packing material, must count. You will need to wrap your treasured evacuation items in something else treasured or useful which can do double duty as the packing material. This radically different method of packing is called evacuation packing.

Posterboard #6

Tell them there are two ways to illustrate the above point. The first method is more suitable for a younger group of women. The hostess who chooses this method should be close friends with her guests and not mind her household objects being used.

Method #1

Divide your guests up into two teams. Their challenge will be to wrap ten items for evacuation in 5 minutes or less. You will have already selected ten similar items for each team. You also will have both traditional and non-traditional wrapping material with these items. Encourage everyone to wrap "outside the box." As each item is wrapped it should be carried to a taped off area on the floor designated as the team's transport vehicle. All items must fit within this space. At the end of 5 minutes have each team unpack their items and count how many useful things they have managed to pack in addition to their evacuation items.

The Wine and Chocolate Evacuation Plan

Method #2
Have an area set up where your guests can view a packing demonstration. You should choose a variety of common objects women want to evacuate (photo albums, jewelry, a painting, a vase, etc.) and evacuation wrap them for your guests.

18. A brief discussion of an evacuation wardrobe is conducted at this point. The evacuation wardrobe you pack should consist of a versatile skeleton wardrobe which is appropriate for many different occasions and from which you can build should you lose everything. This wardrobe is called the "Sweet 16 of Evacuation Packing". You should now bring out poster board number seven.

Sweet 16 of Evacuation Packing
1. Basic dark suit
2. Black pants
3. Dressy top
4. Dressy black shoes & purse
5. Blue jeans
6. T-shirts (3)
7. Dressy top which would go with blue jeans (2)
8. Smart casual shoes & purse which will coordinate with blue jeans
9. Casual outfits (2)
10. Casual shoes & purse to go with above outfit
11. Complete sports outfit (tennis, yoga)
12. Underwear
13. P.J.'s
14. Lightweight coat or jacket
15. Ball cap
16. One clothing item you can't stand to leave

Posterboard #7

19. Point out that no matter how great an evacuation packer one is many things will have to be left behind? The best way to try and secure the possessions left behind is to identify your home's safe-storage areas and pack things in these areas. Now display poster board number eight.

Qualities needed to be a Safe-Storage Area

- Strong and Heavy
- As Airtight as Possible
- Favorable location in relation to the disaster

Common Safe-Storage Areas within Most Homes

- Refrigerator/Freezer
- Dishwasher
- Washer
- Dryer

Posterboard #8

To demonstrate how easy it is to pack a safe-storage area pack your washing machine with clothing and let your guests time you. Start with several extra large plastic lawn bags. Go to your closet and grab a handful of hanging clothes; put the garbage bag over the entire bundle, and fold it into your washing machine. Continue doing this until the washing machine is full while you are being timed. Everyone will be surprised when you are finished by how quickly you can safely store a lot of clothing.

20. Lastly pass out brown 10x13 mailing envelopes to everyone. Instruct everyone to address these to someone outside the area they can trust to keep the envelope safe for them. Your guests will probably not have the complete addresses of the persons they will be sending the envelope to, but they should

The Wine and Chocolate Evacuation Plan

write someone's name down. I find if a person starts the process of filling out an address they are much more likely to finish. You should encourage everyone to fill this envelope with a few sentimental things which would probably be forgotten in an evacuation. Examples of such objects to send are some of your children's art work and favorite photographs of your pets. These things may sound trivial when compared to vital documents, but should you lose everything they would be a cherished link to your past.

21. Drawing for the grand prize. A good grand prize is a complete supply of evacuation packing items. You could include a box of lawn sized garbage bags, a box of space saver bags, a box of plastic baggies, and a package of index cards, scissors and packing tape. If a really generous hostess you could throw in a bottle of wine and a chocolate bar.

22. Finally, thank all of your guests for coming. Allow some time for anyone who would like to stay a little longer and ask questions.

Chapter 18: 22 Steps to a Perfect Party 135

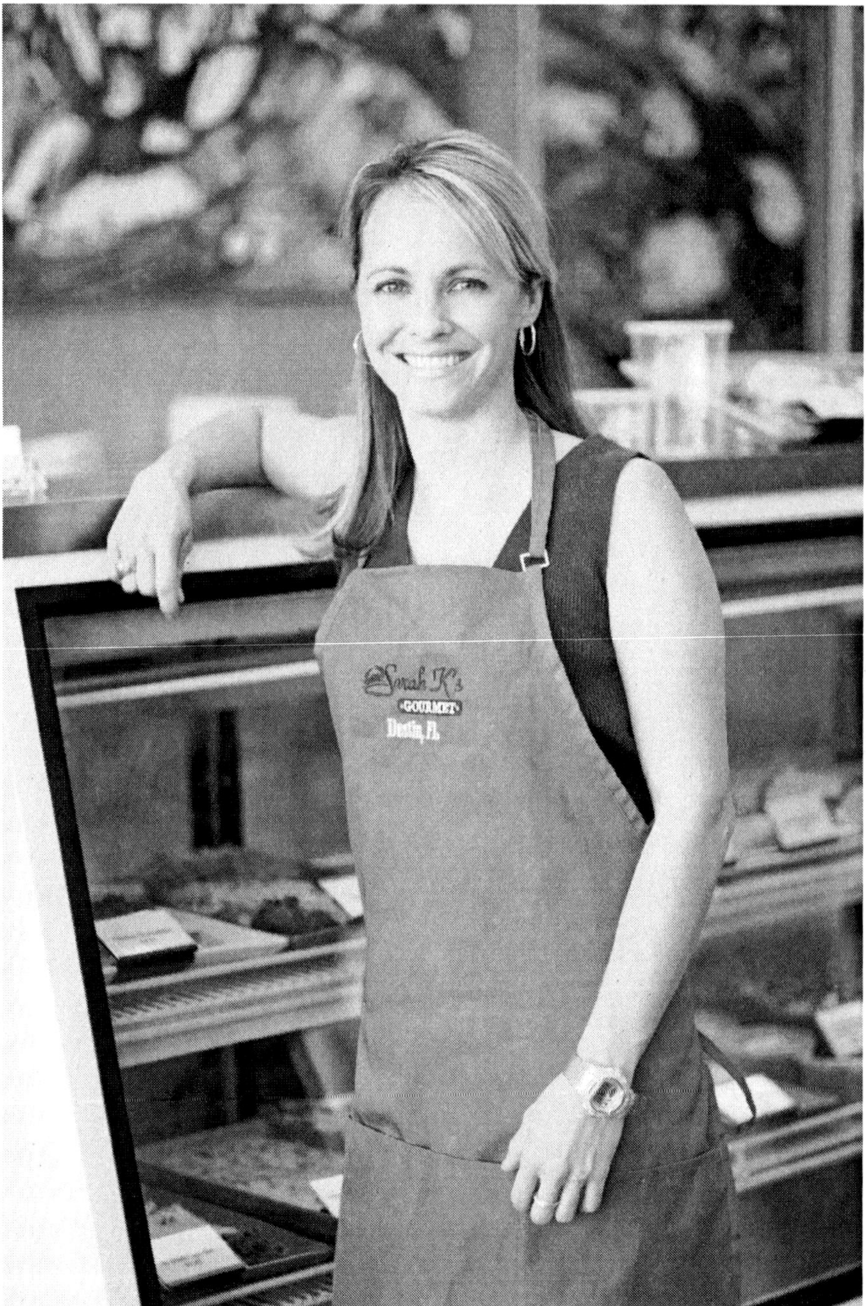
GOURMET

CHAPTER 19

WINE AND CHOCOLATE PARTY MENU

By Sarah K's Gourmet

Ham Dijon Tornado Sandwiches
Miniature buttery croissants filled with Dijon mustard, ham and topped with sesame seeds.

Category 5 Bite Size Chicken Salad Sandwiches
Bite-sized sandwiches with Sarah K's famous chicken salad on freshly baked honey wheat rolls.

Smokin' Signature Spread Platter with Crackers
A special blend of several cheeses, infused with horseradish, served with crackers.

Fire Roasted Inferno Raspberry Spread with Crackers
Raspberry spread with a chipotle kick over cream cheese, served with crackers.

Volcanic Vegetable Platter
Bite size seasonal vegetables with homemade herb dip.

The Wine and Chocolate Evacuation Plan

Quakin' Cupcakes
Miniature chocolate cupcakes topped with blazing fuchsia frosting.

Seismographic Chocolate Strawberries
Plump, juicy strawberries dipped in an assortment of milk, dark, and white chocolate.

Death by Chocolate Bites
Bite size pieces of our most popular dessert.

Monsoon Macaroons
Homemade macaroons drizzled with dark and white chocolate.

RECIPES

Fire Inferno Raspberry Spread

- ½ Cup Raspberry Preserves
- 1 Can of Chiptole in Adobe Sauce
- 8 oz. Philadelphia Cream Cheese
- Crackers

Mix the preserves and adobe sauce. Pour over cream cheese. Serve with crackers.

Volcanic Vegetable Platter with Dip

- 8 oz. tub of Philadelphia Cream Cheese (can be low-fat)
- 1 cup cucumbers, chopped
- 1 carrot, shredded
- 1 green onion, chopped
- ½ clove of garlic, minced
- ½ teaspoon dill weed
- ½ teaspoon lemon juice

Mix all ingredients and refrigerate. Serve with freshly washed and peeled vegetables (baby carrots, celery, cauliflower, etc.). I also like to include asparagus spears and sugar snap peas.

Monsoon Macaroons

- 3 cups (lightly packed) sweetened shredded coconut
- ¾ cup sugar
- 6 egg whites only from large eggs
- 1 ½ teaspoon vanilla extract
- ¼ teaspoon vanilla extract

Topping
- 9 ounces of bittersweet or semisweet chocolate (not unsweetened)
- 6 tablespoons heavy whipping cream
- ¼ teaspoon vanilla extract

Mix coconut, sugar and egg whites in a large, heavy saucepan. Cook over medium heat until mixture appears somewhat pasty; stirring constantly, about 12 minutes. Spread coconut mixture on a large baking sheet lined with parchment. Refrigerate until cold, about 45 minutes.

Preheat oven to 300 degrees. Line another baking sheet with parchment. Press ¼ cup (use more or less depending on how large you want the macaroons) into a pyramid shape-about 1 ½ inches high and place on prepared sheet. Repeat. Bake 30 minutes or until golden. Let cool.

Mix the chocolate and cream in a very heavy saucepan over medium heat until melted and smooth. Remove from heat. Stir in vanilla extract. Invert cookies and dip in chocolate. Place cookies upright on baking sheet and refrigerate until set.

Variation: You can also drizzle white chocolate over the finished macaroons.

The Wine and Chocolate Evacuation Plan

Seismographic Chocolate Strawberries

- 6 oz. semisweet chocolate, chopped
- 3 oz. white chocolate, chopped
- One pound of strawberries, washed and completely dry

Place the semisweet and white chocolate in two separate glass bowls. Fill 2 saucepans with a couple inches of water and bring to a simmer over medium heat. Turn off the heat, set the bowls of chocolate over the water (bowls should not touch the water) and stir until smooth.

Alternatively, melt the chocolates in a microwave at half power, stir and heat for another minute of until melted. You may need to add a few drops of vegetable oil to the chocolate.

Once the chocolates are melted and smooth, remove from the heat. Hold the dried strawberries by the stem and dip into the melted chocolate. Be careful to not get chocolate on the stem or the leaves. (You can use either chocolate first depending on your preference). Dip the fruit into the chocolate and twist slightly, letting any excess chocolate fall back into the bowl.

Place the dipped strawberries on a cookie tray lined with parchment paper. Dip a fork in the other color of melted chocolate and drizzle the chocolate over the dipped strawberries.

Let the strawberries sit for 30 minutes until the chocolate is set. To force the chocolate to set, place in the freezer for no more than three minutes.

Quakin' Cupcakes

- ¾ cup self-rising flour
- 2/3 cup all purpose flour
- ½ cup unsalted butter, softened
- 1 cup sugar
- 2 eggs
- ½ cup milk

Frosting
- ½ cup unsalted butter, softened
- ¼ cup milk
- 1 teaspoon vanilla extract
- 1 drop red food coloring
- 3-4 cups confectioners' (powdered) sugar

Preheat oven to 350.

Cupcakes:
Line 12 mini muffin tins with mini muffin papers. In a small bowl, combine flours. In another bowl cream the butter and sugar until fluffy. Add eggs and beat well. Add flour mixture a little at a time until you have added half. Then add milk and vanilla, beating all the while. Add the remaining flour mixture and beat until fully incorporated. Fill the mini muffin tins ¾ full. Bake 10-15 minutes until a toothpick inserted in the center comes out clean.

Frosting:
Beat butter, milk, vanilla, food coloring and 2 cups confectioners' sugar on medium speed until smooth and creamy. Gradually add remaining sugar until light and fluffy. Pipe or spread the frosting on the cooled cupcakes.

The Wine and Chocolate Evacuation Plan

GROCERY LIST

I have provided the food supply list required to prepare the above recipes. The grocery items are arranged according to the section of the market where they can be located.

Produce
    Strawberries-1 pound
    Lemon-1/2 teaspoon
    Garlic-1/2 clove
    Green Onion-1
    Carrot-1
    Cucumber-1
    Asparagus Spears-1 package
    Baby Carrots-1 package
    Celery-1 package
    Cauliflower-1

Baking Supplies
    Self-Rising Flour-3/4 cup
    All Purpose Flour-2/3 cups
    Sugar-1 ¾ cups
    Vanilla Extract-3 ¼ teaspoon
    Red Food Coloring-1 drop
    Confectioners' (Powdered Sugar)-4 cups
    Dill Weed-1/2 teaspoon
    Almond Extract-1/4 teaspoon
    Bittersweet or Semisweet Chocolate-9 ounces
    Semisweet Chocolate-6 ounces
    White Chocolate-3 ounces
    Sweetened Shredded Coconut-3 cups
    Parchment Paper
    Mini Muffin Pan and Papers

Refrigerated Section
Milk-3/4 cup
Eggs-6 large
Heavy Whipping Cream-6 tablespoons
Unsalted Butter-1cup
Philadelphia Cream Cheese-8 ounce package & 8 ounce tub

Can Goods and Staples
Raspberry Preserves-1/2 cup
Crackers-1 box
Chiptole in Adobe Sauce-1 can

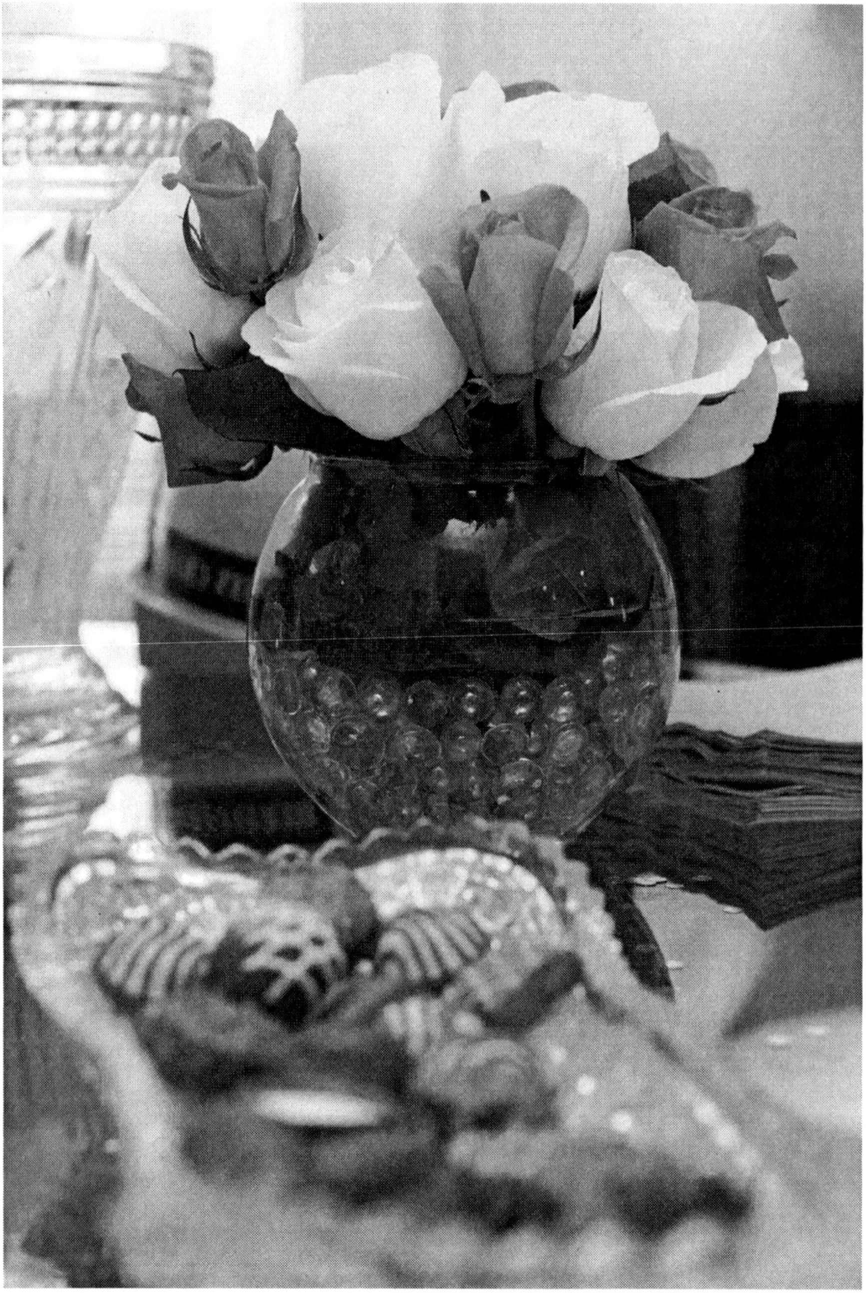

CHAPTER 20
DECORATIONS

The decorations for your party should be a reflection of your taste and personality. The following are some decorating ideas I have used which do not require a great amount of money or skill.

I put extra effort into the wrapping of the two prizes to be given away and use them as decorations. The grand prize (tower of bright pink boxes festooned with ribbons and the book) will not be given away until the end and can be a colorful focal point for the party.

I love fresh flowers but I am not skilled at arranging them. I find it easier and more cost effective to stick with one type of flower which I gather in small to medium sized vases.

Most house plant and their pot can be placed into a bright pink plastic bowl to coordinate with the party color scheme.

Any clear container (vase, glass, candy dishes, goblets, etc.) can be filled with bright pink or white objects to add to the decorations. A quick and easy table centerpiece is to fill a tall clear vase with two bright pink feather boas and let the ends of one of the boas spill down the sides of the vase. I finish decorating the table by scattering a package of sparkling pink confetti over the tabletop.

The Wine and Chocolate Evacuation Plan

Balloons can be an affordable option for party decorations. I often order a dozen balloons in bright pink and silver or bright pink and white colors. I will then place a balloon bouquet at my front door and tie the remaining balloons individually around the party area.

Chapter 20: Decorations 147

SHOPPING LIST FOR 12 PARTY GUESTS

1. Bright pink paper and envelopes for the invitations
2. Stamps
3. 10 bottles of wine (I estimate 3 glasses per guest and 1 bottle to be given   with the grand prize). You will know your guests tastes and may be able to adjust this amount.
4. Chocolates
5. Bright pink cocktail napkins and paper plates
6. Balloons
7. 12 index card notebooks
8. 42 yards of pink ribbon 1 inch wide
9. 12 pencils and pens
10. 2 boxes of gallon sized zip lock baggies
11. 2 boxes of space saver bags
12. 1 box of lawn sized garbage bags
13. Packing tape
14. 3 packs of index cards
15. Scissors
16. CD with some kind of storm sounds
17. 1 case of bottled water
18. 1 package of 10x13 mailing envelopes
19. Food supplies (see separate list)
20. 8 bright pink poster boards
21. A black marker
22. 2 copies of The Wine and Chocolate Evacuation Plan to give as prizes
23. 12 whistles on lanyards
24. 12 small flashlights
25. 12 tape measures

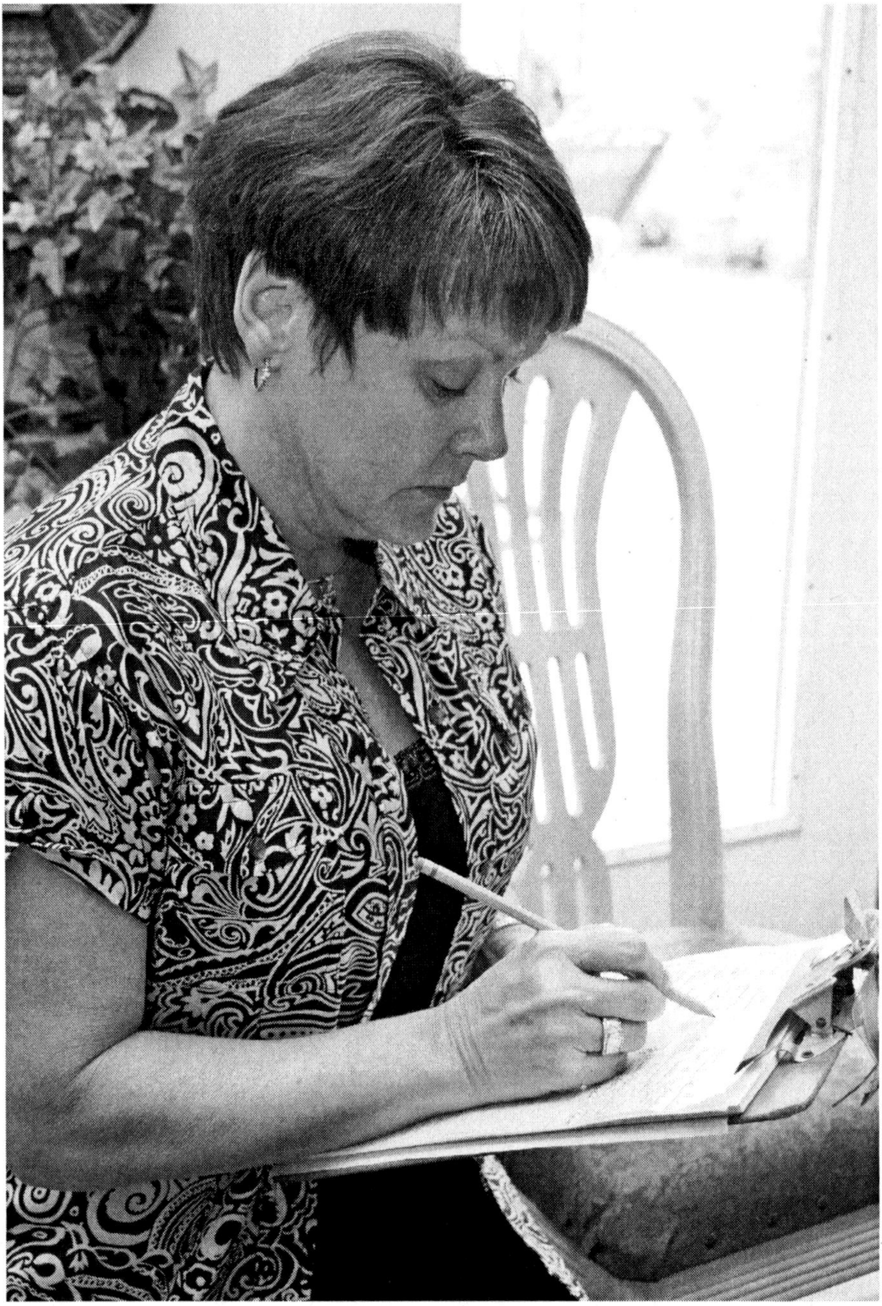

EVACUATION CHECKLIST

A step-by-step guide for an actual emergency.

Okay the plan and party time are over, a natural disaster is approaching and you are really going to have to evacuate. You are probably feeling rushed and overwhelmed. These feelings are normal given the situation, but you can do this. If you are reading this, you are already more prepared than most people. Slowly take a long deep breath; calm down; and focus on the following instructions. I will not have time to tell you why I want you to do something but I will be able to tell you what you need to do.

1. Decide where the evacuation destination will be and how you and those with you will get there.

2. Figure out how long it will take you to safely reach this destination. (Remember to take your normal travel time and multiply by three.) This time estimate is important because it dictates when you must leave and how much time you have to prepare.

3. Prepare the vehicle you are leaving in for the trip. Whichever mode of transportation is carrying you to safety (car, truck, boat, airplane) should be full of fuel, in good repair, and its

The Wine and Chocolate Evacuation Plan

storage area should be cleaned out and ready for packing into.

4. Keep your family and pets close to you. You should dress your children and yourself in bright colors. Small pets should be placed in their carriers and large animals need to have their collars put on and their leashes nearby.

5. Get some cash which needs to be divided and placed in different locations. Some cash should go in your bra and some should be placed in the purse you are taking. If you are traveling with another trustworthy adult, you might ask them to carry some cash for you.

6. Keep your car keys on your body at all times during and after the evacuation preparation process.

7. Gather your important papers. There is a list of what you need on page 33 of this book.

8. Pack your top ten evacuation items. If you have your evacuation deck filled out these items are already chose; their location listed; and their packing labels prepared. If you have not filled this out, and you cannot decide what to take, turn to the list of the most commonly evacuated items on page 129 and pack those things. Please use the evacuation packing method we went over. The packing material you use must be something which would be useful following a disaster (sheets, towels, extra clothing, etc.)

9. Load all of these wrapped evacuation items in your vehicle.

10. Pack clothing for yourself and anyone else you are responsible for. You should use the sweet sixteen of evacuation packing, located on page 66, as your packing guide.

11. Load all of the clothing into the vehicle. At this point pause and evaluate how much space is left in your storage area. If

there is still room available, continue evacuation packing and loading until the space is completely filled.

12. Secure the items which must be left behind. You should start by cleaning out the refrigerator and freezer. Throw out all ice, ice cream, and old food and move anything you want to save to the bottom of the freezer or refrigerator. The ice maker needs to be shut off. You can now fill this empty space with anything you value but are not able to evacuate. I recommend wrapping the stored items in plastic garbage bags to help protect them. If you have a box of baking soda open the top and place it inside.

13. Utilize the space inside your dishwasher as a safe storage area. Any dishes, glassware, or china objects would be good choices to place inside. After loading everything inside be sure to lock the dishwasher door.

14. Identify and pack inside any other household items which are appropriate receptacles. Possible suggestions are washing machines, dryers, heavy dressers and chests, closets, and car trunks. It is important to consider how vulnerable this packing space would be to the disaster. Do not pack in a low area if a flood threatens. Do not store things in a car trunk if wildfires are approaching.

15. Unplug all major appliances.

16. Close every single door throughout your house.

17. Take the very best book, wine, and chocolate you have and leave for the evacuation destination. I want you to depart with a peaceful mind knowing that you have done your best.

The Wine and Chocolate Evacuation Plan

In Conclusion

I have a great idea that you should put in your book.

I have been fortunate to meet many women who had clever, innovative ideas about evacuations. Repeatedly these women told me, "I have a great idea that you should put in your book." Then they would tell me about their experiences, and their idea to improve the evacuation process. Many of these women were smart and generous.

I would like to invite anyone else who would like to contribute an idea or story for future editions of this book to contact me at www.wineandchocolateplan.com, or at the address below. Thank you in advance for your suggestions.

> Brenda Barnes
> P. O. Box 382
> Destin, Florida 32540-0382

The Wine and Chocolate Evacuation Plan

The Wine and Chocolate Evacuation Plan

The Wine and Chocolate Evacuation Plan